8/a
12/c
M
10d

80

150
as is

C0-DAQ-277

INDIAN ART

An unabridged and unaltered reprint of the
original edition which first appeared in
conjunction with the Royal Academy's
historic exhibition of Indian art held in
the Winter of 1946–7.

INDIAN ART

essays by

H. G. RAWLINSON

K. de B. CODRINGTON

J. V. S. WILKINSON

and

JOHN IRWIN

edited by

Sir Richard Winstedt

K.B.E., C.M.G., F.B.A., D.LITT.

OCTOBER HOUSE INC.

NEW YORK

This edition published 1967 by
October House Inc.
134 East 22nd Street
New York, N.Y. 10010
Copyright © *1966 by Sidgwick and Jackson Ltd*
All rights reserved
Library of Congress catalogue card no. 67-10788
Printed in Great Britain

CONTENTS

[5]

INDIA :

THE
HISTORICAL BACKGROUND

*

H. G. RAWLINSON, C.I.E.

INDIA :

THE HISTORICAL BACKGROUND

THE INDUS CIVILIZATION

If we except the palæolithic and neolithic finds in central and southern India, the history of Indian culture may be said to start with the remarkable discoveries made at Mohenjo-daro, near Larkhana in Lower Sind, in 1922. The so-called Indus civilization covered a wide area, extending as far north as Rupar on the Sutlej at the foot of the Simla hills, and as far west as Baluchistan and the Makran. Who the people were will probably remain a matter of controversy until we discover the clue to the pictographic inscriptions on the Mohenjo-daro seals, but from the evidence of the pottery they seem to have arrived, probably about 2500 B.C., by way of the Mula Pass and the coastal road which runs through Las Bela and the Makran, and crosses the Hab river near Karachi. They appear to have been an intrusive race of Sumerian origin. Sind was not then the arid desert of later times, but a fertile country like lower Bengal, inhabited by the elephant, the rhinoceros, the tiger and several species of deer. Wheat and cotton were cultivated.

The Indus folk were townsmen, and excavations at Mohenjo-daro have laid bare an extensive city. The streets are wide and at right angles. The houses, built of dried brick, were several storeys high, with an elaborate drainage system. The most interesting feature is a large public bath, 39 feet by 23 feet, with steps leading down to the water and ingenious arrangements for filling and emptying it. Just to the south of it is a large building, 200 feet long and 100 feet wide, which may have been the royal palace. No temple or place of worship has so far been found.

The people were highly artistic, and the most charac-teristic finds have been a large number of seals or amulets of steatite, finely engraved. Pottery, turned on the fast lathe and highly burnished, was fine and varied in type. It is ornamented with black bands, and, more rarely, with figures of birds, animals and trees. Sometimes the decoration takes the form of clay knobs. The Indus folk were skilled metal workers, and the finds include beakers, knives, spears and swords, and a socketed bronze axehead of fine workmanship. Jewellery was as popular as in later India, and necklaces consisted of beads of gold, faience, jadeite, amazonite, lapis lazuli and carnelian.

What brought about the fall of the Indus civilization is uncertain. It may have been caused by a climatic change, an alteration in the course of the Indus, malaria, or an invasion by more virile tribes from the north and west. Or it may have been due to a combination of all these factors. There is evidence that Mohenjo-daro was sacked, but excavations on other sites seem to show that the decline was a gradual one, and there was possibly a migration to the east in search of fresh homes.

ARYANS AND DRAVIDIANS

The earliest event in India of which we have any literary evidence is the migration into the north-western Panjab, from about 1500 B.C. onwards, of a fair-skinned people, closely akin to the Old Persians, who called themselves Aryans or Nobles. They came in successive waves, accompanied by their wives and families, their flocks and their herds. Our knowledge of them is derived from the Vedic Hymns, the earliest known compositions in any Indo-Aryan tongue, put together when the Aryans were still dwelling in scattered communities between eastern Afghanistan and the Ambala district. As time went on, they were driven, probably by the pressure of fresh waves of invaders, into the territory between the Ganges and the Jumna. This became the *Aryavarta,* the Aryan country; the Panjab receded into the background, and the Ganges replaced the Indus and its tributaries, the Five Rivers, as the sacred stream.

We can fòrm a fairly clear picture of primitive Aryan society from the Vedas. Government was patriarchal. The father was the head of the family; a number of families made up the tribe, at the head of which was the king, who led it into battle. The nobles fought from chariots, like the Homeric heroes, and the chief weapon was the bow. When the people were not fighting or hunting, their favourite occupations were listening to the family bard and gambling with dice.

The Aryan pantheon consisted of gods of the upper air, akin to those of Homeric Greece—Dyaus pitar (Jupiter), the Sky Father, the Moon, the Dawn, Agni the Sacred Fire, and Indra, the Indian Thor, wielder of the thunder-bolt, who led the Aryans in battle. Neither images nor temples formed part of Aryan worship, for the gods were never clearly anthropomorphized. The altar was a cleared space, covered with sacred grass; the fire was kindled with the fire-stick, and fed with clarified butter (*ghi*), while flour cakes, grain and milk were offered, the priest in the meanwhile chanting verses from the Vedas. The sacramental drinking of the intoxicating juice of the Soma plant was an essential part of the ritual.

A further development of Indo-Aryan civilization is

recorded in the two great epics, the *Mahabharata* and the *Ramayana*. The former recounts the struggle between the two rival branches of the royal house, the Pandavas and the Kauravas, for the throne of Indraprastha (Delhi); the latter records the adventures of Rama, prince of Ayodhya (Oudh), while rescuing his bride Sita who had been carried off by the demon-king Ravana to Lanka (Ceylon). A knowledge of these two poems is essential for a proper understanding of Indian culture; like the Iliad and the Odyssey, they form a storehouse of legend, from which later poets and dramatists, sculptors and painters drew their inspiration.

The Aryans were not unopposed in their advance into the Indian plains. They encountered strong opposition from the earlier inhabitants, who are described in the Vedas as dwelling in walled cities, black in colour and 'noseless' and practising phallic worship and other offensive rites. The Aryans termed them Dasyus or Dasas (slaves) and it is commonly supposed that they were Dravidians or Tamils, now confined to the country south of the Godaveri river. One result of the clash was the rise of the caste-system, which originated in a colour-bar (*varna*). Later, caste was occupational; the conquerors devoted themselves to war, hunting and the worship of the gods, leaving the more menial occupations to the subject races. Later on, the Aryans, who were comparatively few in number, settled down and intermarried with the people of the country, and absorbed much of their culture and habits. A. K. Coomaraswamy and others have pointed out that the main elements in Hinduism are of Dravidian origin. Among them are the worship of Siva Mahadeva (the Great God *par excellence*), the cults of the phallus and the mother goddess, Nagas, Yakshas and other nature spirits, and the shift from

[12]

absolute symbolism to anthropomorphic iconography. 'To the Dravidians are probably due the forms of architecture based on bamboo construction; the architecture of the Toda hut has been cited as a prototype or at any rate a near analogue of the early barrel-vaulted *chaitya* hall and horseshoe arch. . . . The stone slab construction of many early temples is likewise of Dravidian (dolmen) origin.'[1] To these Dravidian elements may be added the doctrine of *karma* and rebirth, now the central core of Hindu religious philosophy. It was unknown in the Vedic Hymns, which depict the soul of the dead man as departing to the 'fathers', where it will be judged by Yama, the king of the lower world. The theory of metempsychosis first appears in the post-Vedic philosophic treatises known as the Upanishads. 'Just as a man acts, just as he behaves, so he will be born again,' says the *Brihadaranyaka Upanishad*. Besides this belief there was the doctrine of the World Soul or Atman, of which the individual soul is a fragment or emanation, and into which it will be ultimately absorbed.

BUDDHISM AND JAINISM

By the sixth century B.C., Hinduism had developed into a complicated and jealously guarded ritual, the secret of which was known only to the Brahmins. This led to the rise of two great reform movements started by members of the Kshattriya or warrior caste, and it is significant that they originated in Magadha, or southern Bihar, where Brahmanical influence was still comparatively weak. These were Mahavira the Jain and Gautama Buddha. They were contemporaries, and had much in common. Both taught the doctrine of salvation by works;

[1] A. K. Coomaraswamy, *History of Indian and Indonesian Art*, p. 9.

[13]

liberation from rebirth could be obtained, not by penance and sacrifice, but by right belief, right thought, right speech and right action. Jainism was, however, more extreme than Buddhism, which taught the doctrine of the Middle Way.

The life of Gautama is of vital importance to students of Indian iconography, as it is depicted in endless variety upon Buddhist monuments. Born probably in 563 B.C., the son of a petty chieftain at the town of Kapilavastu on the Nepalese border, he early conceived a disgust for worldly pleasures, and mounting his horse, rode out in quest of the Truth. This was the Great Renunciation. After practising penances and austerities to no purpose, he found illumination while sitting in meditation under a *pipal* tree at Bodh Gaya. Henceforth he was the Buddha, the Enlightened One. Hastening to the sacred city of Benares, he set the Wheel of the Law revolving by his first sermon in the Deer Park. The rest of his life was spent in preaching, with a little band of disciples, in the villages of Bihar, until, at the advanced age of eighty, he passed away at the town of Kusinagara (483 B.C.). After death, his body was cremated, and the ashes were distributed among his followers and enshrined in *stupas* or dome-shaped burial mounds in various parts of the country. During the Buddha's lifetime, considerable political changes occurred in north-eastern India. The various petty states and tribal republics were absorbed in the empire of Magadha, with its capital at Pataliputra, the modern Bankipore near Patna, now the capital of Bihar.

THE MAURYAN EMPIRE

Meanwhile, important events were taking place in north-western India. In 516 B.C. Darius overran the north-western Panjab, and for over two centuries this part of the country was under Persian rule, with far-reaching cultural results. In 327 B.C. Alexander of Macedon, having overthrown the Persian empire, sailed down the Indus to its mouth, subduing the various Indian tribes which he encountered, and setting up Greek governors. On his death at Babylon in 323 B.C. the Greek garrisons were expelled in a national rising prompted by a young man from Magadha of the name of Chandragupta (Sandracottus), of the Mauryan family, who afterwards deposed the reigning monarch at Pataliputra, and made himself master of his kingdom. Chandragupta subsequently defeated an attempt by the Greek ruler, Seleucus to repeat Alexander's exploits, but made a close alliance with him and received a Greek princess into his harem. The long and intimate connection of north-western India with Persia, and subsequently with Greece, has a significance which must not be overlooked.

The first foreign account of India is from the pen of Megasthenes, the Seleucid ambassador who was attached for many years to the court at Pataliputra. The Mauryan capital was well laid-out, with broad streets and handsome bazaars where indigenous and foreign goods were displayed for sale. Buildings, like those in Burma, Kashmir and parts of southern India to-day, were of timber and brick, and the use of stone was unknown. The royal palace had wooden pillars, exquisitely carved, and plated with gold and silver, ornamented with designs of vines and birds. 'In the Indian royal palace,' says Megasthenes, 'there are wonders with which neither Memnonian Susa in all its glory, nor the magnificence of Ecbatana can hope to vie.' Trade was in a flourishing condition, and was aided by the excellent system of roads connecting the capital with the northern trade routes on the one hand, and the ports on the west coast on the other. 'Silks, muslins, the finer sorts of cloth, cutlery and armour, brocades, embroideries and rugs, perfumes and drugs, ivory and ivory work, jewellery and gold (seldom silver) were the main articles in which the merchant dealt.'[1]

A landmark in Indian history was the conversion to Buddhism of Chandragupta's grandson, Asoka. Asoka came to the throne in 273 B.C. and in 261 the imperial armies overran the mountainous country of Kalinga or southern Orissa; 150,000 people were slain, 100,000 made prisoners, and many more perished of disease and famine. Remorseful at the suffering he had caused the Emperor embraced the Buddhist creed, and renounced war and the use of violence throughout his domains. This was an event of outstanding importance, for Buddhism rose from the position of an obscure sect to that of the official religion of a vast empire, covering the greater part of India.

The conversion of Asoka coincides with the employment of stone in place of wood for architecture and sculpture, and this is a turning-point in the history of Indian art, for the King, with the convert's zeal, erected a large number of monuments to commemorate his newly-found faith. These chiefly took the form of edicts graven on rock-face for the edification of his subjects, and huge monolithic columns of highly polished sandstone which were erected at various spots connected by tradition with episodes in the life of the Buddha. Asoka's magnificent palace was still standing six centuries later, when the Chinese pilgrim, Fa-Hian, visited Patalipatra. Fa-Hian recorded his conviction that it must have been

[1] *Buddhist India*, by Rhys Davids, p. 98.

[16]

the work of spirits, who piled up the stones, reared the walls and gates, and executed the elegant carving and inlaid sculpture-work in a manner which no mortal hands could accomplish.

Asoka is credited with the erection of no less than 84,000 *stupas* to enshrine relics of the Buddha in various parts of the empire, but none of these have survived. The group of *stupas* at Sanchi, in the State of Bhopal, so skilfully restored by Sir John Marshall, must be attributed to the Sunga dynasty, which succeeded the Mauryas about 185 B.C.

To a rather earlier period belongs the great *stupa* at Bharhut, not far away to the south. It has not fared so well as those at Sanchi, and only the eastern gate and portions of the railing have survived. They have been re-erected in the Calcutta Museum. Here the bas-reliefs on the medallions and the male and female figures of spirits acting as door-guardians at the entrance to the sanctuary have an archaic naïvety which is singularly pleasing. The *torana* or gateway is also much simpler in style, and the whole structure is generally of a more primitive type than the Sanchi group.

THE KUSHAN EMPIRE

The scene now changes once more to the Panjab, where a succession of foreign invasions, by Bactrian Greeks, Sakas and Parthians, culminated in the establishment of the Kushan empire. The Kushans were a branch of a Central Asian tribe, the Yueh-Chi, and the greatest of their rulers was Kanishka (A.D. 120–62). Kanishka's capital was at Peshawar, and his dominions included Kashmir, the Panjab, Mathura and the Ganges-Jumna delta. Kanishka became a convert to Buddhism, and like

Asoka, was an ardent patron of that religion; but the Mahayana Buddhism of the first century A.D. was very different from the simple ethical creed of the Mauryan Emperor. Buddha was no longer a dead teacher, but a living Saviour God, the last of a long series of incarnations (Bodhisattvas) for the redemption of the human race. The sculptors of Sanchi and Bharhut had a puritanical objection to the representation of the Master in human form; his birth was symbolized by a lotus-flower, his conversion by a *bodhi* tree, his first sermon by the wheel of the law, and his death by a *stupa*. Kanishka and his contemporaries had no such scruples, and Greeks from Asia Minor were employed to decorate the *stupas* and monasteries of Gandhara in the north-western Panjab with figures of the Buddha and representations of episodes in his life. The appearance of the Buddha image marks a revolution in Indian iconography. While retaining Indian characteristics, he is stylistically Hellenic; his features are Greek rather than Indian, and he wears his monk's robes draped in the Græco-Roman manner.

The Gandhara sculptures, which may be seen in large numbers in European museums, are mostly in dark grey slate. At Hadda and other sites in Afghanistan, there developed, about the fifth century A.D., a later school to which Sir John Marshall applies the term 'Indo-Afghan', which appears to be an offshoot of Gandhara and embodies many of its traditions. Lime composition takes the place of stone as a medium, and the faces are cast in moulds. Scenes from the life of the Master are replaced by idealized Buddhas and Bodhisattvas, with portrait figures of donors and monks. It persisted until all traces of Buddhism in the district were obliterated by the devastating Hun invasions in the sixth century A.D.

Contemporary with Gandhara, an indigenous school

of sculpture arose at Mathura on the Jumna river, an important commercial and religious centre. The Chinese pilgrim, Fa-Hian, who visited it about A.D. 410, said that Mathura contained twenty monasteries and upwards of three thousand Buddhist monks. The studios at Mathura supplied Buddha images which were exported in great quantities to Sarnath and other religious centres in the Ganges region. The earliest known Buddha figure from Mathura was a colossal statue excavated at Sarnath in 1904, which was dedicated by the monk Bala in the third year of Kanishka.

THE GUPTA DYNASTY

After the death of Kanishka, the Kushan empire gradually declined, and the next dynasty of which we have any definite information is that of the Guptas. A chieftain bearing the historic name of Chandragupta, having married a princess of the powerful Lichchavi clan, managed to extend his dominions over the Gangetic plain as far as Allahabad, and was crowned according to Brahmanical rites in A.D. 320. He was succeeded by his son Samudragupta, a powerful prince who subdued most of the independent principalities of northern India, but was unable to penetrate south of the Narmada river. About A.D. 380, the Gupta monarch Chandragupta II transferred the seat of government from Pataliputra to Ayodhya, the chief town of Kosala or Oudh, and the court seems to have spent part of its time at the ancient city of Ujjain.

The Guptas were Hindus by religion but freely patronized other religious sects, and Buddhism in particular continued to flourish. The Chinese traveller Fa-Hian, already quoted, gives a glowing picture of what he saw on his visit to the country. The inhabitants were prosperous and happy, and taxation was light. The roads were good, and the country was covered with monasteries which served as rest-houses for pilgrims and as centres of learning. At Pataliputra was a hospital maintained by charitable contributions, where the destitute, sick and crippled of all countries were treated free of charge. Education reached a high standard, and mathematics, astronomy and medicine were among the subjects studied. Orthodox Brahmanism was busy codifying its laws. Classical Sanskrit reached its zenith under royal patronage, and to this period belong the group of dramatists known as the 'Nine Gems'. The greatest of them was Kalidasa, whose masterpiece, the world-famous *Sakuntala,* was performed in the presence of the court at the Spring Festival of Ujjain.

Hindu sculpture attained a new peak of perfection under the Guptas. Structural temples began to be erected, and the panels on the walls of the ruined shrine at Deogarh in the Jhansi district, depicting scenes from the *Ramayana,* reach a standard hitherto unattained. The clumsy coarseness of the Mathura sculptures of the Kushan period has vanished, and the Hellenistic influence inherited from Gandhara has been completely absorbed. A European scholar has said that 'the Gupta period is in the annals of classical India what the Periclean age is in the history of Greece'.

The Gupta dynasty seems to have been brought to an end by the Hun invasions at the end of the fifth century A.D., and after a blank period the curtain rises upon the short-lived splendour of the court of Harsha of Thanesar on the Ganges, who came to the throne in A.D. 606, and made himself master of northern India after six years of incessant fighting. We are fortunate in possessing accounts of this monarch by the Sanskrit romance writer Bana, and by the Chinese pilgrim, Hiuen Tsiang, the Master of the Law, who spent eight years in Harsha's dominions. Harsha moved his capital to Kanauj, not far from Lucknow, and the pilgrim had the privilege of witnessing two religious festivals, one at Kanauj and the other at Prayaga (Allahabad), at the junction of the Ganges and Jumna, which is still the scene of an annual pilgrimage. At the one, a golden image of the Buddha on a gorgeously caparisoned elephant was carried in procession by twenty subject kings. At the other, Harsha, imitating the good prince Visvantara in the *Jataka* story, in successive days gave away all his wealth to Brahmins and religious mendicants.

Learning was held in high esteem. The king himself was an excellent scholar, and like the emperor Akbar at a later period, presided at religious debates, his widowed sister, a very learned lady, seated by his side. Hiuen Tsiang gives an interesting account of the university of Nalanda in Bihar, at which he studied for some years. 'The whole establishment is surrounded by a brick wall. One gate opens into the great college, from which are separated eight other halls, standing in the centre of the quadrangle. The richly-carved towers and fairy-like minarets cluster like pointed hill-tops; the upper storeys and observatories are lost in the morning mists. . . . All the outside courts, in which are the priests' chambers, are of four stages. The stages have carved and coloured eaves, pillars and balustrades, and the tiled roof reflects the light in a thousand shades.' The lecture rooms were over one hundred in number, and the resident students from all parts of Asia often exceeded ten thousand. Recent excavations on the site have confirmed the general accuracy of Hiuen Tsiang's description.

THE RAJPUTS

The death of Harsha in A.D. 647, as always happens in India when the hand of the strong ruler is removed, plunged the country into chaos. The Hun invasions were resumed, and a curtain descends upon the scene. When it rises once more, it is upon a greatly changed India. Hindustan is divided into a number of kingdoms, ruled over by warlike clans calling themselves Rajputs or Sons of Kings. They claimed descent from the ancient Kshattriya caste of the days of the Indian epics, but modern research has proved that they actually originated from Huna, Gurjara and other central Asian tribes, whose leaders had obtained admission into the Hindu fold. They quickly developed into a haughty and exclusive aristocracy, living in fortified castles surrounded by hosts of retainers. Much may be learnt about them from that great storehouse of Rajput legend, Tod's *Rajasthan*. The Rajput's main occupation was war, and the old ballads give a vivid picture of the warriors passing the night before the battle listening to recitations from the *Mahabharata* and longing for the morning as a lonely wife longs for her husband. An important person was the bard, who was the repository of the unwritten history of his clan and a herald in time of war. Women held a high place in Rajput society; the princess chose her husband from among her suitors, and when he died in battle, the true wife (*Sati*) passed through the fire with her lord. When a besieged fortress was on the point of capture, the ladies immolated themselves by the terrible *jauhar* rite, rather than fall into the hands of the enemy, and the men sallied out to meet death by the sword.

The Rajputs were great builders, and there is no more picturesque part of India than Rajputana. The Palace of the Winds at Udaipur and Man Singh's palace at Gwalior are striking examples of domestic architecture, and the great fortresses of Jodhpur and Chitor remind the spectator of the strongholds of mediæval Europe. The Mughal emperor Babur, who had a pronounced dislike for everything Indian, was struck with admiration at these buildings. 'They are singularly beautiful,' he notes in his memoirs. 'The domes are covered with plates of copper gilt. The outside of the wall is inlaid with green-painted tiles. All round they have inlaid the walls with figures of plantain trees made of painted tiles.'

Mention must also be made of the Pala and Sena dynasties which ruled over Bengal and Bihar from A.D. 750 until they were swept away by Muhammadan invasions at the end of the twelfth century. Under the Palas, sculpture and working in metal attained a high degree of proficiency. The names of two famous craftsmen, Dhiman and his son Bhitpalo, who were equally proficient in casting, stonework and painting, are recorded. The highly stylized figure of the Sun God, Surya, in black carboniferous shale, now in the India Museum, South Kensington, is typical of the Pala period.

In the meantime, a highly ornate type of architecture was appearing in western India, chiefly under the patronage of the Solanki rulers of Anahilvad. At Mount Abu in southern Rajputana is a group of Jain temples, dating from the eleventh and thirteenth centuries, which are celebrated for what Fergusson calls 'the lace-like delicacy of the fairy forms into which the patient chisel of the Hindu has carved the white marble.'

THE KINGDOMS OF THE DECCAN

The Deccan or South Land comprises the great plateau which lies to the south of the Narmada river and the

Vindhya mountains. It was part of the country visited by
Asoka's Buddhist missionaries, and its earliest rulers, the
Andhra kings, patronized the Buddhist religion. The
Andhra kingdom was extremely prosperous. On the west
coast lay a number of ports which maintained a flourishing
commerce with Alexandria and the Persian Gulf, and
good roads ran from them to various parts of the interior.
A feature of Andhra economy was the powerful trade
guilds, which were liberal in their donations to the
religious orders, and this, no doubt, accounts for the
large number of *viharas,* or rock-hewn dwellings for
Buddhist communities, which are found along the main
trade-routes. The excavation of these dwellings was,
as Fergusson points out, really more economical
than the erection of buildings, which involved the
quarrying and cutting of stone, and carrying it for long
distances over bad roads. Each *vihara* has its *chaitya* hall or
chapel, used by the community for purposes of worship;
the most striking example of this is at Karle, on the high
road running over the Bhor Ghat from Bombay to Poona.
This noble structure is 45 yards long and 15 yards in
width, with a spacious nave and two side aisles. The
ribbed roof is supported by stone pillars, and in the apse
is a massive *stupa*. It is lighted by a large horseshoe-shaped
window over the entrance, and at the sides of the door
are portraits of the royal donors. The whole effect is not
unlike that of an early Christian basilica, with the *stupa*
taking the place of the altar.

Few remnants have survived of the open-air *stupas* which
were at one time numerous all over Andhra domains;
the most important must have been the monument at
Amaravati at the mouth of the Kistna river, erected by
King Pulumayi II (A.D. 138–70). Remains of another *stupa,*
with richly carved architraves and panels, were discovered

at the neighbouring site of Nagarjunikonda in 1927.

The break-up of the Andhra kingdom in the third century A.D. was followed by a period of confusion, until the country was consolidated three centuries later under the rule of the powerful Chalukyas of Badami, who were in their turn succeeded by the Rashtrakutas in A.D. 757. During this period, cave-temples reached their zenith in the elaborate Ajanta and Ellora caves, both situated in the state of Hyderabad, which has done admirable work for their preservation. Fresco painting had long been in fashion for decorative purposes, and 'picture halls' are frequently referred to by the classical dramatists. Caves XVI and XVII at Ajanta are square halls supported on massive columns, which provide a large wall space. Both walls and ceiling are decorated with brilliantly executed frescoes representing episodes from the life of the Buddha, Jataka stories and court scenes. The mural paintings of the Bodhisattvas Avalokitesvara and Maitreya in the antechamber of Cave I are justly famous. The Ajanta caves are the latest and most splendid monuments of Buddhist art in India.

The Ellora caves, not far from the city of Aurangabad, are Buddhist, Jain and Brahmanical. The Buddhist and Jain caves are elaborately carved, the *stupa* usually being ornamented with a figure of the Buddha or Jaina; the florid decoration of these caves contrasts strongly with the noble simplicity of the *chaitya* at Karle. The most remarkable of the edifices at Ellora, however, is the Kailasa[1] temple commenced by the Rashtrakuta king Krishna I (A.D. 757–800). To the same period belongs the great Hindu cave temple on the island of Elephanta in Bombay harbour, with its majestic three-headed figure of the Indian Trinity, Brahma, Vishnu and Siva.

[1] Kailasa is the Indian Olympus.

With the decay of Buddhism and the rise of orthodox Hinduism, the structural temple was beginning to replace the *chaitya* cave in the Deccan, though, with his usual conservatism, the Hindu mason at first modelled it with as little departure as possible from traditional architectural forms. The numerous temples of the southern Deccan are in what has been called the Chalukyan style—long, low buildings with a squat, dome-like tower over the *garbha* or shrine, in striking contrast to the lofty steeples of the Indo-Aryan type in the north. The Chalukyan style reached its climax in the time of the Hoysalas of Mysore in the twelfth and thirteenth centuries, when the splendid shrines at Belur and Halebid were erected.

THE PALLAVAS

Mention must here be made of the Pallavas, probably an indigenous race originally feudatories of the Andhras, till they asserted their independence on the break-up of the Andhra empire. From A.D. 550 to 750 they were the ruling power in southern India, their territories including what are now the districts of Arcot, Chingleput, Trichinopoly and Tanjore. Their capital was at Kanchi (Conjeeveram), and Hiuen Tsiang describes it as a great centre of learning, with a number of monasteries for Buddhist and Jain monks. The Pallavas were the traditional enemies of their neighbours, the Chalukyas, against whom they carried on a series of ferocious wars. About the middle of the eighth century A.D. they were absorbed in the Chola empire, and this brought to an end one of the most brilliant and interesting of the southern dynasties.

The most characteristic works of art of the Pallavas

are the series of small monolithic temples known as the Seven Pagodas, standing on the seashore, and carved from single granite boulders. The history of architecture and sculpture in Southern India begins at the close of the sixth century A.D. under Pallava rule.

THE CHOLAS

In the far south the leading dynasty was that of the Dravidian Cholas, which reached its climax under the rule of Rajaraja the Great (A.D. 985). The Cholas maintained a fleet which dominated the Bay of Bengal, and like the Pallavas they carried on endless wars with their neighbours the Chalukyas. They were great builders and knew how to dam rivers and construct vast reservoirs for irrigation purposes. The Cholas were bigoted Hindus, and the famous Hindu religious reformers, Sankaracharya (A.D. 788) and Ramanuja (A.D. 1100) both came from southern India, and were responsible for stamping out the heretical Buddhist and Jain sects. A feature of Dravidian India is the vast, cathedral-like temples, built in the form of a square and enclosing a tank or pool. These temples have lofty gateways (*gopuram*) covered with carvings, which dominate the flat landscape for many miles. The single block of stone forming the summit of the gateway at Tanjore is said to weigh 80 tons, and in order to place it in position, a ramp 4 miles long had to be erected. Southern India produced some important bronzes; the best known is the Siva Nataraja, of which there are examples in the Madras Museum and the India Museum, South Kensington, and there are representations of the Tamil Saivite Saints.

[27]

THE MUHAMMADAN INVASIONS

The rise of Islam was one of the most extraordinary events in the world's history. Muhammad was fifty years of age before he was joined by any followers outside his family circle. The people of his native city of Mecca were so hostile that he had to flee to Medina: this was the year of the Hijra or Flight, A.D. 622. He died ten years later, and his successors, the Caliphs, led the Arabs to the conquest of the neighbouring countries. Within a hundred years they had spread as far as North Africa in the west, and Asia Minor and Persia in the east.

Baghdad, under the Caliph Harun al-Rashid, succeeded Alexandria as the great international centre of culture, where learned men resorted and exchanged ideas from all over the world. Indian books were translated into Arabic, and in this way many Indian folk-stories, as well as Indian treatises on mathematics and astronomy, found their way to Europe by way of Spain. Sind was overrun by the Arabs, but their advance westward was barred by the great desert and by the strong Parihar kingdom of Kanauj. They were on friendly terms with the Hindu rulers of Gujarat and the Deccan.

After a time, however, power passed from the Arabs into the hands of the fierce Turki races of Central Asia. In A.D. 991, Sabuktigin, the ruler of the little mountain kingdom of Ghazni, invaded the Panjab, and after defeating a confederacy of Rajput princes led by a prince named Jaipal, captured the frontier town of Peshawar. His successor, Mahmud of Ghazni, made annual raids into northern India, returning to the mountains at the end of the cold weather laden with booty and driving before him hordes of prisoners, who included skilled craftsmen for the decoration of his capital. In A.D. 1018, he took the sacred city of Mathura, which contained a temple dedicated to Krishna of almost incredible splendour. In it were five idols of red gold, each 5 yards high, with priceless rubies for eyes. These were carried off, and the edifice was razed to the ground.

But the most famous of Mahmud's exploits was his raid, over the trackless desert sands, on the celebrated temple of Somnath (Siva, Lord of the Moon), which stood on the sea-shore on the southern extremity of the penin-sula of Kathiawar. It was one of the most famous places of pilgrimage in India, and contained a stone *lingam,* 5 cubits high, which was washed every day with Ganges water and garlanded with flowers from Kashmir. The inner shrine, like many in ancient India, was built of wood. It was supported by fifty-six wooden pillars, coated with silver and encrusted with jewels. A chain of golden bells hung over the idol, which was lighted by chandeliers of the same precious metal. The temple, with its hordes of ministrants, formed a regular town, surrounded by a series of massive fortifications.

Mahmud left Ghazni in December 1023, and appeared before the walls of Somnath at the end of the following month. Next day the assault began. The Hindus fought desperately, calling upon the god to come to their help, but were driven back inch by inch with fearful slaughter. At length the inner defences were stormed; 50,000 Brahmins were put to the sword, and the plunder exceeded 2,000,000 *dinars.* The priests offered large sums in order to ransom the *lingam,* but Mahmud refused to spare it, saying that he was a destroyer and not a seller of idols, and it was broken into pieces which were buried in the threshold of the great mosque at Ghazni, to be trodden underfoot by true believers.

THE DELHI SULTANATE

Mahmud of Ghazni died in 1030, and in 1150 Ghazni was overthrown by the ruler of a neighbouring principality, Muhammad of Ghor. India, which for fifty years had enjoyed a respite, was now subjected to fresh invasions. The Rajputs, led by Prithvi Raj Chauhan, in 1191 collected a mighty host which awaited the invader at Tarain, the plain outside Delhi where the fate of India has so often been decided. The Hindus were completely defeated, and most of the Rajput strongholds were captured. The survivors took refuge in the inaccessible deserts of Rajputana.

In 1199, the Muhammadans began to move eastward. Bihar was overrun by Muhammad Bhaktiyar. The country was still largely Buddhist by religion, and, as its name implies, covered with monasteries. The 'shaven-headed monks' made little resistance, and the survivors fled to Tibet and Nepal. The famous university at Nalanda, with its vast library of Buddhist and Hindu books, was destroyed. The Muhammadans next entered Bengal, and overthrew the aged monarch Lakshamana Sena. A Muhammadan capital was set up at Gaur. In 1206, Muhammad Ghori was assassinated by a fanatic, and his viceroy, Kutb u'd-din Aibak (the Pole-star of the Faith) became first Sultan of Delhi. He was originally a Turkoman slave, and his dynasty is popularly known as that of the Slave Kings.

Between 1302 and 1311, Malik Kafur, a eunuch who had been a Hindu slave, made a series of plundering raids into southern India. The Yadava kingdom of Deogiri and the Hoysala kingdom of Mysore were overturned, and the great Hindu temple at Madura was plundered. Malik Kafur penetrated the Tamil country as far as the southern extremity of Cape Comorin and the island of Rameswaram between Ceylon and India, where he erected a mosque. His army returned to Delhi with immense plunder, which included 300 elephants, 20,000 horses, and 2,750 pounds of gold.

It seems at first sight incredible that so vast a country as India should have been conquered by a comparatively small body of invaders with so little resistance. But the reasons were in reality not far to seek. The strength of Islam lies in its doctrine of brotherhood; all Muslims, whether noblemen or slaves, are equals in the sight of God. The Hindus on the other hand were divided into innumerable castes and sects, of which only the Kshattriyas or Rajputs looked upon making war as their concern. The peasants took little interest in a change of rulers, provided that they were unmolested, and moreover, general *morale* was undermined by Buddhist and Jain pacifist doctrines, by a vegetarian diet, enervating climatic conditions and malaria. They were no match for the hardy and reckless invaders from the northern uplands, reared in a cold climate, who considered India as a *dar u'l-harb,* or land of warfare, and the extirpation of idolatry as a religious duty. The Hindu armies were vast undisciplined hordes, and reliance was mainly placed on elephants, which were quite unable to stand up to the mobile horsemen of their opponents, who, like the ancient Parthians, rode round their flanks, pouring in volleys of arrows at close range. This caused a stampede, which was quickly changed into a rout by a frontal cavalry charge.

The Delhi Sultanate lasted for over three centuries (A.D. 1206–1526); the Slave Kings were succeeded in turn by the Khiljis, the Tughlaks, the Saiyyids and the Lodis. The earlier invaders had been absorbed, but the Muslims, like the English after them, remained a people apart. The Hindus were treated as a subject race, and were not allowed to carry arms, ride on horseback, or practise their religion, and were subjected to the humiliating *jizya* or poll-tax on infidels. As time went on, however, these asperities were gradually softened. Inter-marriage became commoner, and low-caste Hindus embraced Islam to escape the tyranny of the caste-system. Some learnt Persian and rose to positions of trust. A *lingua franca* known as Urdu, or the language of the camp, sprang up. There was even a religious synthesis. The Persian sect of mystics known as the Sufis held the Vedantic doctrine that 'God is One, though the Wise call Him by many names'. In the fifteenth century a saint named Kabir, originally a Muhammadan weaver, gathered a body of Muslim and Hindu disciples, and attacked openly the beliefs of orthodox Muhammadanism and Hinduism alike. 'The gods are of stone; Rama and Krishna are dead and gone, and the Vedas are idle tales. God dwells neither in temple nor in mosque.' His contemporary, Nanak, the founder of the Sikh sect in the Panjab, sought to abolish the caste-system and idolatry, and amalgamate Muslim and Hindu in a common creed:

> *Make Love thy mosque, Sincerity thy prayer-*
> *carpet, Justice thy Koran,*
> *Modesty thy circumcision, Courtesy thy Kaaba,*
> *Truth thy teacher,*
> *and Charity thy creed and prayer.*

EARLY MUSLIM CULTURE

The Muslim invaders, fanatical bigots though they were, were cultured people, and patrons of art and literature. Mahmud of Ghazni adorned his capital with fine buildings, many of them the work of Hindu craftsmen carried off in his raids. Among the writers at his court were Firdausi, author of the celebrated epic, the *Shah Nama* or Book of Kings, and the learned historian Albiruni.

The Muslims were not allowed by their religion to practise sculpture, but they made up for it by the elaborate calligraphy which they used to adorn their mosques and tombs with Quranic texts. They introduced into Indian architecture important new elements, the true arch, the dome and the minaret. The result was the evolution of the Indo-Saracenic style, which became characteristic of northern India. For the decoration of their edifices Hindu craftsmen were employed, and materials from Jain and Hindu temples were incorporated. The earliest Islamic monument is the Kuwwait u'l-Islam mosque, built in 1193 to commemorate the capture of Delhi. It is supported on richly carved columns, and enclosed in a colonnade with a lofty arch. The beautiful Alai Darawaza, with its gateway of red sandstone and marble, was added in 1311. Most of the architecture of the period is severe and rather forbidding; a typical example is the tomb of Tughlak Shah, with its plain, sloping, fortress-like walls and almost Egyptian solidity. All these, however, are dwarfed by the stupendous Kutb Minar, the work of Sultan Altamsh (1211–36) which dominates the country for many miles around. It is 238 feet high, with fluted storeys, the lower ones red sandstone and the upper marble, tapering gradually to the summit.

THE KINGDOMS OF BENGAL, GUJARAT AND THE DECCAN

During the time of the Sultans of Delhi, the outlying provinces were ruled by their representatives, and in the absence of central control these gradually asserted their independence. In Bengal, two such principalities sprang up at Gaur and Jaunpur; both were adorned with mosques of the primitive type, with solid and imposing gateways and no minarets. Jaunpur was a handsome city, and was popularly known as the 'Shiraz of the East'. The Muslim rulers of Bengal, being few in number and widely separated from Delhi, associated freely with their Hindu subjects, and encouraged the growth of the vernacular language of the country; adaptations of the *Ramayana* and the *Mahabharata*, are the earliest literary works in the Bengali language.

The fertile province of Gujarat, with its important seaports, in great demand by those making the pilgrimage to Mecca was originally conquered in 1297, and became an independent kingdom under its governor, Muzaffar Shah, in 1401. Its capital city, Ahmadabad, was founded by his grandson, Ahmad Shah. It is described as the most beautiful and prosperous city of its time, and was famous for its weavers in cotton, silk and gold and silver thread. Its mosques, with their tall, slender, turreted minarets, its palaces and step-wells, all built from the local yellow sandstone, make Ahmadabad one of the most attractive places in western India. Particularly noteworthy is the delicate tracery of the windows of the Sidi Sayyid mosque, which are masterpieces of the stonecutter's art. The Sultans of Gujarat built mosques at many other places, the most imposing being that at Champanir, now in the state of Baroda.

The most famous of the Gujarat Sultans was Mahmud Bigarha, who was renowned for his personal strength and was the subject of many legends. He carried on incessant campaigns against the Rajputs of central India. His successor, Bahadur Shah, captured Chitor from the Rana of Mewar, but the line of succession was kept alive by the escape of the young prince, Udai Singh, who was smuggled away to a place of safety. Meanwhile, the Portuguese appeared on the scene: they had established themselves at Goa, in the territory of Bijapur, in 1510, and their powerful fleet interfered greatly with the trade of the Indian Ocean. After the middle of the sixteenth century, the sultanate of Gujarat gradually declined, until it was absorbed into the Mughal empire by the emperor Akbar in 1554.

In 1347, an Afghan officer named Hasan Gangu Bahmani set up an independent kingdom in the Deccan, with its capital at Gulbarga, now in the Nizam's dominions. The Bahmani kingdoms at one time ruled over an extensive area of country, stretching from sea to sea. In 1422, the capital was transferred to Bidar. Bidar is still covered with the remains of what was once a magnificent city; particularly remarkable is the Muslim college or *madrasah* built by the celebrated minister Mahmud Gawan, which still stands. It is three storeys high, with spacious lecture-halls, quarters for professors and students, and a library which once held 3,000 volumes. Urdu literature was encouraged, and patronized by the court, as Hindu converts to Islam found it more easy to assimilate than Persian. The government was not unduly oppressive, and a mixed race grew up as a result of inter-marriage between the Muslims and the earlier Hindu inhabitants. An attempt was made by means of irrigation to mitigate the horrors of famine, which was almost endemic in the Deccan in pre-British days. All offices were in the hands of Muslims, but the peasantry were not interfered with. A new feature in the architecture of the time is the appearance of massive stone battlements and bastions, which was due to the introduction of artillery,

[35]

probably as a result of contact with the Portuguese. The principal fortress of the period is the extraordinary stronghold of Daulatabad near Aurangabad. This is a sugar-loaf hill 600 feet high, with a broad and deep moat, scarped sides, and a triple enceinte of loopholed walls; on the summit is a giant piece of artillery which commands the approaches in every direction.

The Bahmani kingdom finally broke into five states, which, after varying fortunes, were eventually absorbed into the Mughal empire; these were Bidar, Golkonda, Berar, Ahmadnagar and Bijapur. Of these only the last claims the attention of the student of Indian culture. The 'Adil Shahi governors of Bijapur were tolerant and enlightened, and the fifth ruler of the line, Ibrahim II (1580–1626), encouraged Portuguese merchants and artists from Goa to visit his court. The capital, now in ruins, stands on a plateau in the southern extremity of the Bombay presidency between the Bhima and the Kistna rivers. Its walls are 6 miles in circumference. Its most striking, though not its most beautiful building, is the Gol Gumbaz, the mausoleum of Muhammad Ali Shah, with its great dome, the second largest in the world. More artistically attractive is the Ibrahim Roza, the tomb of Ibrahim II, with its perforated windows and richly decorated walls. Other buildings of note are the exquisite gateway of the Mehtar Mahal, the Asaf Mahal, which enshrined a hair of the beard of the Prophet, and the Sat Manjali or seven-storeyed palace. They were originally adorned with mural paintings. Bijapur fell a victim to the iconoclastic fury of the emperor Aurangzeb in 1686; the last ruler died as a state prisoner in Gwalior, and the city now stands a melancholy shadow of its former splendour.

THE EMPIRE OF VIJAYANAGAR

Vijayanagar, the City of Victory, on the banks of the Tungabhadra river in what is now the Bellary district of the Madras Presidency, was founded, according to legend, by five brothers, as a rallying place for the Hindu religion against the rising tide of Islam. Being in a wild and remote part of the country, it attracted little attention at first, and here gradually congregated Hindu fighting men and refugees driven out of their original homes in all parts of southern India.

Little by little, Vijayanagar became strong enough to declare its independence, and this was aided by the decline of the Bahmani kingdom. It reached the height of its glory under Krishnaraya Deva (1509–29), an enlightened monarch who encouraged foreign visitors to his capital. Vijayanagar owed much of its wealth to its trade with Portuguese Goa. Cæsar Frederici, the Italian traveller, says that the merchandise which went every year from Goa to Beznagar included Arabian horses, velvets, damasks and satins, Portuguese taffeta and pieces of china, saffron and scarlets. These were paid for mainly from the diamond mines in the Vijayanagar territories, which produced stones of great size and the finest water.

Portuguese travellers describe the capital as an immense city, surrounded by seven lines of fortifications, with a population of half a million; the great central road connecting the northern and southern gates was 8 miles long. The streets were well laid out and paved and lined with bazaars, with lofty arcades and galleries. They were crowded with foot-passengers, pack oxen and elephants. The city was supplied with water from a reservoir made by damming the Tungabhadra river, and conveyed by an aqueduct 15 miles in length. Houses and

[37]

temples were all of stone, and a Portuguese traveller, Domingo Paes, thus describes a temple which won his admiration:

'You must know that it is a round temple made of a single stone, the gateway all in the manner of joiner's work, with every art of perspective. There are many figures of the same work standing out as much as a cubit from the stone, so that you could see on every side of them, so well carved that they could not be better done, the faces as well as all the rest, and each one in its place stands as if embowered with leaves; and above it is in the Romanesque style, so well made that it could not be better. Besides this, it has a sort of lesser porch upon pillars, all of stone, and the pillars with their pedestals so well executed that they appear as if made in Italy; all the cross-pieces and beams are of the same stone without any planks or timber being used in it, and in the same way all the ground is laid with the same stone, outside as well as within.'

Painters, sculptors, architects, jewellers and craftsmen of every kind resorted to Vijayanagar from all over the East. The royal palace was exquisitely decorated. One of the halls was completely panelled with ivory, and had ivory pillars carved with lotuses and roses. Well might the Arabian visitor, Abd u'r-Razzak, remark that 'the city is such that eye has not seen nor ear heard of any place resembling it on earth'.

The wealth and splendour of this rich and famous Hindu city excited the jealousy of its Muslim neighbours, which was increased by the contempt with which they were treated by the haughty Hindu raja, and in 1564 they combined to overthrow it. The immense and unwieldy army of Vijayanagar moved out to meet its opponents at Talikota on the river Kistna in January

1565. It was commanded in person by the aged monarch, Rama Raja, carried in a golden litter as he was too old to mount his war-elephant. The Muslims had the advantage of possessing 600 cannon, cast in the foundries at Ahmadnagar. These were loaded with copper coins, and fired into the closely packed Hindu ranks with devastating effect. The rout was completed by a cavalry charge.

Had the gates of the city been closed and the walls manned, the enemy might yet have been repelled; but a wild panic arose, and the pursuers entered at the heels of the beaten army. The plunder was so great that every private man became rich in gold, jewels, tents, arms, horses and slaves, as the Sultans left every person in possession of what he had acquired, only taking the elephants for their own use. The conquerors then went to work with axe and crowbar and fire until they had reduced the city to a ruin. So vast was the city that it took five months to complete the work of destruction. A visitor who reached the site a few years later found it a mere shell, inhabited only by tigers and wild beasts.

THE MUGHAL EMPIRE

The founder of the so-called Mughal empire was Zahir u'd-din Muhammad, surnamed Babur (Tiger), a Barlas Turk who claimed descent from Timur on his father's side and Chingiz Khan on his mother's. His early life and adventures are graphically described in his inimitable *Memoirs*. Born in the little central Asian state of Ferghana in 1482, he set out at the age of fifteen with a handful of followers to capture Samarkand, which had been the capital of his ancestors. But he was expelled by a rival faction, and after wandering 'like a king on chessboard', in 1504 he finally made himself master of Kabul.

But even Kabul did not satisfy him. Inspired by tales of Timur's exploits, he determined to invade India. A quarrel had broken out between Ibrahim Lodi, the Sultan of Delhi, and the governor of the Panjab, which provided him with a pretext for intervening, and in 1525 he marched against Delhi with a tiny force of 12,000 men. The Sultan, a rash and inexperienced young man, awaited him on the plain of Panipat, on April 26th, 1526.

Babur made a lager of wagons lashed together, with cannon and matchlocks mounted on tripods in the gaps. When the Delhi troops attacked, Babur employed the usual Turki manœuvre of enveloping the enemy's flanks by means of mounted archers. It was completely successful, and the Sultan and 15,000 of his men were left dead on the field. The following day, Delhi and Agra opened their gates, and the *khutba* or bidding prayer was recited in the mosques in the name of Zahir u'd-din Muhammad, the first of the Great Mughals.

But fresh perils awaited Babur. He was isolated in the midst of a hostile country, far from home, and his men, who disliked the heat and dust of the Indian plains, were showing signs of disaffection. The Rajputs, who thought that the conflict between the rival powers had weakened the Muslim hold on the country, gathered a mighty host to drive out the intruder. It was led by Rana Sanga of Mewar, the hero of countless fights, who had lost an eye and an arm in battle, and was said to bear on his body the scars of over eighty wounds. Babur told his men that this was a *jihad* or Holy War, and they must conquer or die. Many of them had been in the habit of drinking wine, contrary to the precepts of their religion, but now they poured out their wine on the ground, and breaking their drinking vessels, swore an oath on the Koran that, if they survived, they would never offend again. The two armies met at Kanua, outside Agra. Babur repeated his previous tactics, with the same result as before. The battle raged all day, but at nightfall the Hindu army broke and fled, and for many miles the ground was strewn with countless bodies, jewelled head-dresses, silk scarves and richly inlaid weapons. In three more battles, Babur reduced all northern India to submission. He was now the master of an empire stretching from the Oxus to the Ganges. It was divided into provinces, each under an officer responsible for law and order and the collection of revenue, and for supplying troops when called upon. The Hindu nobles who submitted were left undisturbed.

Babur hated India. Its people, he said, were ugly and devoid of refinement and artistic sense, and the country was no better. There were 'no good horses, no good flesh-meat, no grapes or melons, no ice or cold water, no good food or bread, no baths or colleges'. He spent his remaining years in trying to make Agra resemble his beloved Samarkand, with marble baths, pavilions and watercourses. He died in December 1530, at the age of forty-eight, but he had packed into his few short years the adventures of a long life. He had been fighting since the age of twelve, 'a king for thirty-six years crowded with hardship, tumult and strenuous energy'. He was a born leader, brave and chivalrous, and a lover of beauty in nature and art. His body was taken for burial to Kabul, where it lies in a garden on a hill outside the city, surrounded by streams and under the shadow of the delectable mountains. His grave was marked a century later by a delicate marble tomb, erected by the orders of his descendant, the emperor Shah Jahan.

Babur's son and heir, Humayun, was a drug addict, and quite incapable of maintaining order. The Afghan nobles began to throw off the yoke, and in 1540, he was driven into exile by Sher Shah, the governor of Bihar. While he was a fugitive in Sind, his wife gave birth to a son, the future emperor Akbar, at the fortress of Amarkot. He afterwards took refuge in Persia, where he was hospitably received by Shah Tamasp.

Sher Shah proved to be an excellent ruler, and during his short reign of five years, he introduced many reforms. The nobles were reduced to obedience, and excellent roads were built, which greatly strengthened the power of the central government. Hindus were freely employed, and were allowed to practise their religion. The land was surveyed, and the amount of revenue to be paid by the peasants was laid down. Village officers were made responsible for maintaining order, and it was said that 'an old woman with a pot of gold might securely lay herself down beside her burden, even in the desert'.

Sher Shah was unfortunately killed in 1545 in an explosion of gunpowder, and was buried beneath a stupendous mausoleum at Sahasram in Bihar; Humayun then returned from Persia, only to die as the result of a fall in the following year.

At the time of his father's death, Jalal u'd-din Akbar was only thirteen years old, and his guardian Bairam Kahn hastily arranged for his enthronement before rival claimants should arise. The only resistance came from a Hindu named Hemu, who seized Agra and Delhi and tried to restore the Hindu Raj. He was defeated on the field of Panipat and put to death. In 1560 Akbar, now eighteen years old, determined to shake off the interference of the regent, Bairam Khan, and the other courtiers who kept him in leading strings. He found himself, however, almost alone, and the Afghan nobles, who hated the Mughals, were seeking an opportunity to rise.

By a masterly stroke of policy, he decided to enlist the support of the Rajputs, who had been treated by the Delhi Sultans as a conquered race. For this purpose, in 1562, he married a Rajput princess, the daughter of Raja Bihar Mal of Jaipur, and abolished the hated *jizya*, or poll-tax on Hindus. The Rana of Mewar, who refused to submit, was defeated, and his great stronghold, the fortress of Chitor, was captured. Gujarat was conquered in 1572, and Bengal two years later.

In 1586, Kashmir was annexed and became the summer resort of the Mughal court. In 1600, the Deccan was invaded and Ahmadnagar submitted. This left Akbar master of a stupendous empire, stretching from the Oxus to the Godaveri river. It was divided into fifteen *subas* or provinces, each under a Subadar or Viceroy, a great noble and a member of the imperial family. But no office was allowed to become hereditary. The Suba was divided into Sarkars or districts, administered by Mansabars, who were both military and civil officers. For revenue purposes, Akbar employed a clever Hindu of the name of Todar Mal, who completed the work begun by Sher Shah. The Mughal system of government instituted by Akbar was substantially that followed by the British when they conquered India.

The sixteenth century was an age of religious ferment all over the world, and Akbar, like Henry VIII in England, was determined to free himself from ecclesiastical influence and be head of the Church (*Imam-i-'adil*). He had doubtless learnt something about Hinduism from his Hindu wives and friends, and he fell under the influence of Shaikh Mubarak, who was a Sufi, and his two sons, Abu'l-Fazl and Shaikh Faizi. Abu'l-Fazl was the most learned man of his age, and the author of the *Akbar Nama*, or History of the Reign of Akbar. Abu'l-Fazl's

[43]

religious views may be gathered from a verse of one of his poems:

'O God, in every temple I see people that seek Thee: in every
    language that I hear spoken, people praise Thee!
If it be a mosque, people murmur the holy prayer: if it be a
    Christian Church, they ring the bell for love of Thee!
Sometimes I frequent the Christian cloister, and sometimes the
    mosque;
But it is Thou whom I seek from temple to temple.'

In 1579, Akbar issued his Infallibility Edict, in which he claimed the sole right to decide any religious question about which there was doubt, and ascending the pulpit in the Great Mosque, he himself recited the *khutba* or bidding prayer composed for him by his friend Faizi, now poet laureate.

Akbar's great ambition was to find a common religion which would unite India, and for this end he built his famous Hall of Worship (*Ibadat Khana*) for the purpose of holding religious discussions, in which he took a keen interest. He invited Hindus, Jains, Muslims, Zoroastrians and Christians to take part in them. For this purpose, he induced a party of Jesuit missionaries from Goa to visit his court; they came in 1580, bringing with them copies of Italian religious paintings, which delighted the Emperor. They were received with great distinction, and were allowed to build a chapel at Agra. Finally, Akbar, dissatisfied with all creeds, determined to establish an eclectic one of his own, which he named the *Din Ilahi* or Divine Faith. It found, however, few adherents outside his personal circle, and did not survive him.

Akbar's later years were clouded with sorrow, caused by the unfilial conduct of his sons. Two of them, Murad and Daniyal, were vicious and worthless, and died of drink. Salim, the son of the Rajput princess and his father's favourite, lived in open rebellion at Allahabad, and hired an assassin to waylay and murder Akbar's beloved friend and counsellor, Abu'l-Fazl, who died in October 1605.

Akbar lived in an age of great monarchs—Elizabeth of England, Philip II of Spain, Henry IV of France and Shah Tamasp of Persia—and in many respects he transcended them all. 'One could recognize even at first glance that he is a king,' wrote one of the Jesuit Fathers. 'His expression is tranquil, serene and open, full of dignity, and when he is angry, of awful majesty.' His religious tolerance was in striking contrast to the bigotry of contemporary Europe. Though formally illiterate, he was a great patron of poetry, and had a library of 34,000 volumes. He caused Hindu religious books such as the *Bhagavad Gita* to be translated into Persian. He was a patron of painting and music, and liberally encouraged Hindu as well as Muslim artists. Like all the Mughals, he had a passion for architecture, and built Fathpur Sikri, the City of Victory, which was the residence of the court from 1570 to 1585.

Akbar was succeeded by Prince Salim, who took the title of Jahangir or World Grasper. He was very unpopular, and a rising of the younger nobles to place his son Khusru on the throne was barbarously suppressed. Khusru was thrown into prison, where he died, probably of poison. Jahangir married Nur Jahan, the widow of a Persian nobleman. The Empress completely dominated her husband, who was addicted to drink and drugs, and she appeared openly in the Hall of Audience, transacting the business of government in his name. During this reign, William Hawkins visited Agra and obtained from

[45]

the Emperor permission for the English to open a trading factory at Surat. Jahangir was a despicable character, weak, indolent and cruel, but his Memoirs show him to have been intensely artistic and a poet of no mean order. He was especially fond of gardens, and constructed the Shalimar Gardens at Lahore and the Shalimar and Nishat Bagh at Kashmir, to which the Court regularly moved to avoid the heat of the Indian summer.

Jahangir died on his way from Kashmir in 1627, and was succeeded by his son Khurram, who took the title of Shah Jahan or Lord of the World. Shah Jahan started the policy of trying to reduce the independent kingdoms of the Deccan, which was ultimately to prove the ruin of the Mughal empire. Vast sums of money were also spent on magnificent buildings: the Taj Mahal, the splendid mausoleum which Shah Jahan built for his Empress, took twenty years to erect, and cost four million pounds sterling. Even larger sums were lavished upon the Jama Masjid at Delhi, on the huge marble palace, with its lavish inlaid work, and the famous Peacock Throne, its golden pillars encrusted with jewels. This brought the country to the verge of bankruptcy. 'The whole country is ruined,' says the French traveller Bernier, 'by the necessity of defraying the enormous charges required to maintain the splendour of the numerous court, and to pay a large army maintained for the purpose of keeping the country in subjection. No adequate idea can be conveyed of the sufferings of that people. The cudgel and the whip compel them to incessant labour for the benefit of others, and driven to despair by every kind of cruel treatment, their revolt and flight is only prevented by the presence of military power.' A terrible famine broke out in Gujarat, and the starving peasantry were reduced to devouring dogs and cats and even human corpses.

Shah Jahan's sons were, in accordance with the usual practice, made viceroys of the various provinces. In 1657, a War of Succession broke out among them. In the end, the victor was Prince Aurangzeb, who made away with his rivals, threw his father into prison, and caused himself to be enthroned in 1659 with the title Alamgir.

Unlike his predecessors, Aurangzeb was a religious fanatic. His sole aim in life was to purify India of idol-worship and make it a 'land fit for Islam'. Temples were destroyed, and the hated poll-tax re-imposed on the Hindus. The Rajputs, whom Akbar had looked on as the 'sword-arm of the Empire', were deliberately provoked.

Aurangzeb then plunged into a fresh war in the Deccan. He was a strict Sunni, and was determined to reduce to submission the heretical ruler of Bijapur. This he did, but came to blows with fresh opponents, the Marathas, who had risen to power under their ruler Sivaji. The Marathas were hillmen, and experts at guerrilla warfare. They refused to be drawn into a pitched battle, but hung on the flanks of the unwieldy imperial armies, ceaselessly harassing them. At last the old Emperor, worn out by his exertions, died in the field in 1707. He was eighty-nine.

The Empire now rapidly disintegrated. In the north-west, Afghans, Sikhs and Jats were in open revolt. The viceroys of Oudh and Bengal became virtually independent, and a great noble, the Nizam-u'l-Mulk, carved out for himself a kingdom at Hyderabad in the Deccan. The English and French began to establish themselves on the Bombay and Coromandel coasts, and at the mouth of the Hughli. In 1739, Nadir Shah of Persia ransacked Delhi, and carried off the Peacock Throne. In 1803, the poor blind emperor Shah 'Alam, seated under a tattered canopy in his ruined capital, gladly accepted the protection of Lord Lake. The last of the line, Bahadur Shah, was tried for complicity in the mutiny of 1857 and banished to Rangoon, where he died. India then came under the rule of the British Crown.

MUGHAL ART AND CULTURE

With the coming of the Mughals, Indian architecture takes on a new aspect; the solid and massive dignity of the Pathan style is modified by Persian influence. The main innovations were the introduction of the bulbous dome, the lofty vaulted gateway, and rows of cupolas standing on slender pillars. Practically nothing of Babur's age survives, and our knowledge of Mughal architecture begins with Akbar. His work may be studied most easily in the city of Fathpur Sikri, which has survived almost intact. The central feature is the mosque which enshrines the tomb of the Saint, Salim Chishti, in whose honour the city was built. The tomb is of shining white marble, with exquisitely carved lattice-work and mother-of-pearl inlaying; the contrast with the rose-red sandstone of the surrounding mosque is very striking.

There are numerous other buildings of great interest, including the Hall of Audience, with its massive pillar surmounted by a huge capital, from which radiate four railed balconies. The emperor sat in the middle, with his four ministers of state at the four corners. This singular monument is characteristic of the emperor's genius, as, indeed, is everything in the city. All else, however, is dwarfed by the Buland Darwaza, the lofty gateway which is his noblest monument. It was erected to commemorate his conquest of Khandesh in 1601, and it is adorned with the famous inscription:

'Jesus Son of Mary (on whom be peace) said: The world is a bridge; pass over it, but build no house upon it. Who hopes for an hour, hopes for eternity. The world is an hour. Spend it in prayer, for the rest is unseen.'

Among Akbar's other buildings, the great fort at Agra and the tomb of his father Humayun, a tentative essay in a new style, are deserving of particular notice.

The architectural remains of the reign of Jahangir are not numerous; the most important is the mausoleum of Akbar at Sikandra, with its four diminishing terraces, and the white marble tomb of his father-in-law, Itimad u'd-daulah, a graceful monument in white marble, with the *pietra dura* work characteristic of the later period.

Mughal architecture reaches its zenith under Shah Jahan; besides the Taj Mahal, too often described to need further mention, is the vast palace at Shahjahanabad, with its maze of marble chambers, profusely inlaid with *pietra dura*. In the centre lies the Diwan-i-Khas, or Hall of Private Audience, where

> High on a throne of royal state, which far
> Outshone the wealth of Ormus or of Ind,
> Or where the gorgeous East, with lavish hand,
> Showers on her Kings Barbaric pearl and gold. . . .

the Great Mughal, seated on his Peacock Throne, received his nobles and ambassadors from all parts of the world. It is only possible for us to-day, looking upon the remains of departed glory, to imagine the scene as Bernier beheld it:

'At the foot of the throne were assembled all the Omrahs in splendid apparel, upon a platform surrounded by a silver railing, and covered by a spacious canopy of brocade with deep fringes of gold. The pillars of the hall were hung with brocades on a gold ground, and flowered silk canopies were raised over the whole expanse of the extensive apartment, fastened with red silken cords from which were suspended large tassels of silk and gold. The floor was covered with carpets of the richest silk, of immense length and breadth.'

It is a relief to turn from these gorgeous but some-times tawdry oriental splendours, to the Jama Masjid with its grand and simple lines, and the chaste and exquisite simplicity of the Pearl Mosque, which is a gem of beauty unsurpassed in the architecture of the period for grace and elegance.

Painting, which had been regarded by the earlier Delhi Sultans as contrary to the precepts of the Koran, was warmly encouraged by the Mughal Emperors, and Humayun brought back with him from Persia an artist named Mir Sayyid 'Ali, a pupil of the famous Bihzad of Herat. At the same time indigenous schools of painting had developed in Rajputana, Jammu and Kangra. Akbar took a keen personal interest in this branch of art, and took up two Hindu painters, Basawan and Daswanth, whom he had trained in the studio of Khwaja Abdu's-Samad, Humayun's court painter. He was also greatly influenced by the Italian religious pictures brought to Agra by the Jesuit missionaries.

Indian painting reached its highest degree of perfection in the reign of Jahangir, when it was a happy blend of Iranian, Indian and European influences, and the stiff formality inherited from Persia gave way to a charming

[50]

naturalness and freedom from convention. Mughal painting was essentially a court art. The artists were regularly
paid, and employed in illustrating works like the *Akbar
Nama,* and in representing palace scenes, hunting expeditions and portraits of the emperors and the great nobles.
Jahangir, who was a great lover of nature, employed the
artist Mansur to make some exquisite studies of flowers
and animals. Skill in calligraphy was greatly admired, and
very often a painting was the work of three collaborators,
the first being responsible for the border, the second for
the landscape, and the third for the figures. The Hindu
schools, while resembling that of the Mughals in general
technique, chose widely different subjects. They were
usually scenes from Hindu mythology, the loves of
Krishna and the *gopis* being the favourite, and allegorical
illustrations of the *Ragas* or musical modes. Traces of
mural painting are visible at Bijapur, Fathpur Sikri and
other places.

With the accession of Aurangzeb to the throne, a
general decline in the arts set in. Almost the only
buildings that the emperor allowed to be erected were
mosques, and these were plain and unadorned. The use of
gold and silver vessels and even of rich clothes was forbidden. The utmost simplicity of life was imposed upon
the court. Artists and jewellers, who had hitherto thriven
on imperial patronage, were reduced to indigence. In his
youth the emperor had been passionately fond of music,
but now even this was frowned upon. One day, according to a well-known story, a funeral procession was heard
passing the palace. When Aurangzeb enquired whose it
was, he was told that the corpse of Music was being
taken out for burial. 'Bury him deep,' he answered, 'that
not a sound of him comes to my ears.'

THE BRITISH PERIOD

The great anarchy which prevailed all over India between the break up of the Mughal empire and the establishment of British rule was a period of almost universal decline. The decadent architecture of the Court of Oudh at Lucknow shows little trace of the beauty and grace of the Mughal period at its best. Central India was ravaged by bands of Maratha plunderers, who stabled their horses in the palaces and mosques and turned the Taj Mahal at Agra into a dwelling-place. Everything of value was broken up and carried off by these imperial robbers, who even stripped the silver ornaments from the ceiling of the palace at Delhi.

The earlier generation of the East India Company's servants were keenly interested in oriental culture; many of them spoke Persian fluently, and made their home in the country. Warren Hastings, a good orientalist, made a collection of Indian paintings which was afterwards acquired by the India Office, and under his patronage, Sir William Jones, Wilkins, Colebrook and other scholars penetrated the hitherto unexplored secrets of the Sanskrit language, and made them known to European scholars. *Sakuntala* was translated into English, and won the enthusiastic applause of Goethe. Others, like General 'Hindu' Stuart, were connoisseurs of sculpture. Thanks to the 'Nabobs', England became interested in *Chinoiserie*: Indian chintzes, brass and inlaid work became a familiar sight in English homes. Artists from Rembrandt to Sir Joshua Reynolds were admirers of Indian painting.

In 1835, English became the medium of higher education in India, and replaced Persian as the official language. The result was an indiscriminate admiration of everything Western on the part of educated Indians, and a neglect of

[52]

their own unique cultural heritage. The torch was kept alight chiefly by Englishmen. J. Fergusson was the first to make a systematic study of Indian architecture; English archæologists discovered the Ajanta caves, and took the first steps to preserve their priceless paintings from decay. Others rescued from local vandals what was left of the carvings which once adorned the *Stupas* of Bharhut and Amaravati. But the chief credit belongs to Lord Curzon, who in 1904 passed the Ancient Monuments Preservation Act, and brought out Sir John Marshall as the first Director General of Archæology. Under Marshall's supervision, the great Hindu and Muslim monuments of the past were carefully restored, and the group of Buddhist *stupas* at Sanchi in the Bhopal state now stands as it did in the days of its glory, after centuries of neglect. Among Marshall's other outstanding achievements were the excavation of the ancient city of Taxila, the exploration of the Buddhist sites of Sarnath, Bodh Gaya and Nalanda, and the discovery of the lost civilization of the Indus valley.

Indian art had fallen into undeserved neglect in the Victorian era, and a true appreciation of its spiritual meaning was due to the work of two pioneers, E. B. Havell and Ananda Coomaraswamy. Havell, who was Principal of the Calcutta School of Art, had a struggle not only with the local Government but with his own pupils, before he was able to turn them from European models to their own artistic traditions. The result was an artistic renaissance in Bengal, the protagonists of which were Abanindranath Tagore and his brothers and a group of pupils like Asit Kumar Haldar and Nandalal Bose. The Bengal school turned for inspiration to the Ajanta frescoes, Mughal and Rajput paintings and the classical art of China and Japan. Art trends in India to-day are many and varied; some of the younger artists are coming under the

[53]

influence of modern European, especially French, schools, while others, like Jaimini Roy, base their work mainly on indigenous folk traditions.

The ancient arts of sculpture and casting in metal, for which India was so justly famed, seem to be moribund, but the Indian master-mason still survives, and the buildings, religious and secular, which adorn the capitals of many Indian states, show that he can adapt himself to modern conditions. A great opportunity was missed when they were not employed in the construction of New Delhi. The Indian States also keep alive the minor arts such as enamel and *bidri* work, ivory carving, lacquer work, embroidery, weaving, carpet-making and cotton-printing. It may be hoped that the technical ability latent in India will find new avenues of expression in the free political atmosphere of the future.

INDIAN
SCULPTURE

★

JOHN IRWIN

INDIAN SCULPTURE

Though the earliest examples of sculpture found in India take us back nearly 5,000 years to the period of the so-called Indus Valley civilization, it is not until the second century B.C., when the great Buddhist *stupa* was built at Bharhut, that we are provided with data on which to base any clear conception of the history and development of Indian sculpture as a tradition. It is, indeed, generally admitted that archæology during the last half-century, in bringing to light a highly advanced stage of pre-historic civilization in India not previously conjectured, has raised problems of greater magnitude and complexity than any it has solved.

The most striking fact about the discoveries in the Indus Valley and farther afield (the Harappa site being most typical) is that we are confronted with evidence of a culture already long-established and highly conventionalized, with no clues to earlier stages of development and very little indication of its bearing on the subsequent development of art in India. The enormous task of excavating this vast area, where numerous sites have been located, is still in its initial stage; and until financial aid is forthcoming on a scale necessary to overcome the technical and other difficulties involved, it is doubtful if any theories constructed can be more than conjectural.

On the evidence at present available, it is believed that the city-states of the Indus Valley reached the peak of their industrial and commercial development during the third millennium B.C. This date is calculated according to Mesopotamian chronology, certain Indus seals having been discovered at Mesopotamian sites roughly contemporaneous with the latter part of the Early Dynastic Period of Babylonia (c. 2550 B.C.). Connection between the two civilizations is so obvious that it is sometimes questioned if the culture of the Indus Valley inhabitants should be regarded as Indian at all. Yet, allowing for those features of similarity, to be explained by common descent from a much more remote and primitive culture, there is no real evidence of foreign origin. There are, on the contrary, many characteristics of the Indus culture which have no parallel in contemporary Sumer or Egypt, although these three civilizations were based on the same primary technological inventions and discoveries, and it is precisely these distinctive characteristics which stamp the Indus culture as having at least a strong Indian element.

Among the many small fragments of sculpture so far discovered in the Indus Valley, the most æsthetically striking are two mutilated torsos found at Harappa (Plate I, *a*, *b* and *c*). The unique significance of these pieces is that the general features and quality of modelling are far closer to the sculpture of the Hellenistic age, 2,000 years later, than to anything yet found at pre-historic sites in other parts of the world. The first, a statuette carved in red sandstone (Plate I, *a* and *b*), represents the naked torso of a man posed frontally, with shoulders well back and abdomen slightly prominent. The modelling, naturalistic in style, is extraordinarily exact in anatomical detail and shows a sense of volume characteristic of mature sculpture, the surface undulations and the supple flesh being rendered with great plastic subtlety. A surprising feature of technique is that head and arms (now missing) were cut separately and socketed into the torso. Breast nipples, too, were made independently, cement being used to fix them.

The second torso (Plate I, *c*) is carved from grey slate and represents the figure of a male dancer in action. The figure originally stood on its right leg, the left leg being raised high at a transverse angle in front and the body bent well round to counter-balance the swing. The sculptor's aim being to show a body in movement, this piece does not reveal the same studied attention to anatomical detail as the first torso, though modelling and technique are similar. In this case the genital organs as well as the arms and head were made separately for attachment—a detail to which Sir John Marshall ascribes possible ithyphallic significance.[1] The stones employed in these torsos are not found anywhere near the site of excavation, and any attempt to account for the surprising appearance of the two figures would, at the present stage, be mere surmise. There is nothing comparable with them in Indian sculpture until we come to the so-called Græco-Buddhist period some 2,500 years later (second to fifth century A.D.); even so it is doubtful if the fleshy emphasis of the Indus modelling can be paralleled in the muscular treatment of the later style.

Two other Indus statuettes are worthy of special attention for their sculptural qualities. Both found at Mohenjo-daro, they differ radically in style and treatment from each other as well as from the two Harappa torsos. The first (*Figure* 1), a fragment in steatite, 7 inches in height, represents the head and shoulders of a man, the face bearded and moustached, and the body draped with a trefoil-patterned shawl. Here the stylized treatment suggests more obvious—yet only superficial—

[1] *Mohenjo-daro and The Indus Valley Civilization*, by Sir John Marshall (1931) Vol. I, p. 46.

affinities with contemporary Sumerian art, and there are parallel features of technique such as the inlaying of the eyes with shell and the use of a drill for pittings. The

FIGURE I

Statuette found at Mohenjo-daro.
c. 2,500 B.C.

second piece (Plate I, *d*), a bronze casting 4¼ inches in height, is the figure of a dancing girl with legs and arms disproportionately long and the right hand resting lightly on the hip. As an example of *cire-perdue* casting in pre-

[60]

historic times, this piece is of particular interest, and there is a sensuous quality in the modelling more pronounced here than in any of the other Indus finds.

There is a wide variety of terra-cotta figurines, both animal and human, and also many images of what has been taken to be a mother-goddess (*Figure* 2), all of them of a type easily paralleled in other matriarchal cultures. The technique of pinching out the facial features in soft

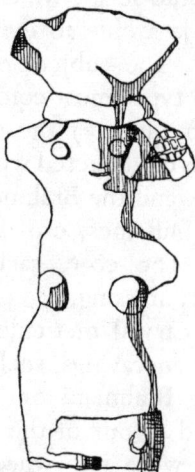

FIGURE 2

Terra-cotta figurine. Mohenjo-daro.
c. 2,500 B.C.

clay and the application of small pellets of clay for such parts as the eyes and breasts are still practised in the villages of north-east India to-day.

Of particular interest are the engravings on the so-called seals or amulets (Plate I, *e*) that have been found in large numbers at the Indus sites. The use of the terms

[61]

'seal' or 'amulet' to describe these small square steatite tablets is purely conjectural, their precise function being unknown. The illustrations usually published are photographs of wax impressions and not of the seals themselves. The majority, but not all of the 'seals', are engraved on one side only and have a small perforated boss at the back, suggesting that they might have been worn round the neck, perhaps as some kind of magic charm. The pictographic script which appears on some, may eventually provide a clue to their use, but has not yet been deciphered. The subject of the engraving is usually an animal, the types most commonly represented being (in order of frequency) the so-called 'unicorn' (thought to be the urus ox depicted with horns in profile), the short-horned bull, and the Brahmani bull. Elephants, rhinoceroses, tigers, buffaloes, crocodiles and antelopes occasionally appear. The cow, sacred animal of the Hindus, is significantly missing.

These animals are carved meticulously in naturalistic detail, and in the best engravings, such as the well-known representation of the Brahmani or 'humped' bull, the majesty and restrained vigour of the beast are strikingly conveyed. The seals were not wheel-cut. Apparently, they were first cut into tablet-shape with a saw and then engraved with a burin. A further interesting clue to the technique is given in Marshall's account of an unfinished seal,[1] from which it appears that the artist began hollowing out the body of the animal before outlining the whole figure, a procedure indicating a tradition of highly specialized craftsmanship.

This brief summary of the salient characteristics of Indus Valley sculpture must suffice here for the sculpture of pre-historic India, further evidence being almost

[1]Marshall, *op. cit.*, Vol. II, p. 43.

entirely lacking. Between this period and the period of the Mauryan Empire, there is an interval of some 2,000 years.

THE MAURYAN PERIOD (322–184 B.C.)

It has already been said that the history and development of Indian sculpture as a tradition does not become clear to us until the second century B.C., a period marked by the construction of the great Buddhist *stupa* at Bharhut. From the remains of the preceding century, however, it is possible to trace the existence of at least two distinct sculptural styles, each of formative significance for subsequent development. On the one hand, we have the Asokan pillars and capitals, the products of a developed and traditional art in which strong Perso-Hellenic influence is said to appear; and on the other, a number of large human statues (of which only four are in any clearly recognizable state of preservation) suggesting the co-existence of a less mature, indigenous school of sculpture.

The Mauryan Empire, founded from the chaos of the Greek collapse, reached its height under Asoka (273–232 B.C.) when its territories stretched across the whole of north and central India, incorporating Afghanistan, Kashmir and the Deccan, and extending as far south as the Narbada river in Mysore. Asoka adopted Buddhism as a state religion. During the two centuries that had passed between the death of the Buddha and Asoka's conversion, Buddhism had been one among many heretical movements challenging Brahmin authority and priestcraft. In proclaiming the equality of man and calling on the individual to seek perfection in his own way, irrespective of caste or convention, and without resort to priestly ritual, the Buddhist gospel had already contained within

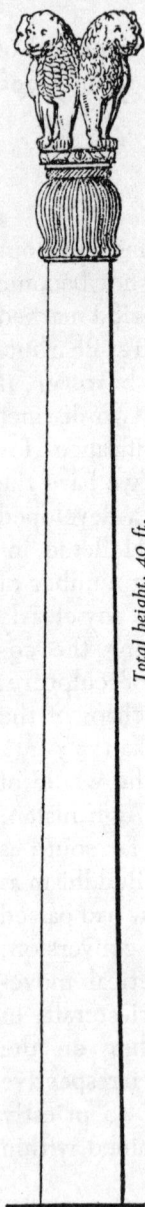

Total height, 40 ft.

itself the seeds of a new liberal humanism admirably suited to the intellectual needs of an age of expanding commerce. Moreover, a centralized bureaucratic administration of the Mauryan type required its universal law or code of conduct: Asoka's *dharmavijaya*, or 'conquest through *Dharma* (Buddhist Law)', in meeting this need, was not merely a missionary movement but a definite imperial policy.

The columns named after Asoka are large monoliths of polished sandstone (*Figure* 3), inscribed with his edicts propagating the *Dharma* or Law. Rising to an average height of about 40 feet from base to summit, they are designed as self-contained monuments to stand in open space, unrelated to any larger architectural unity. The capital of each pillar, like the shaft, is monolithic and incorporates a so-called Persepolitan bell (named after its supposed Persian prototype) surmounted by an abacus and a crowning sculpture in the round (Plate II, *c*). The subject of their finial is usually the lion, bull or elephant, represented singly on the early capitals, but grouped on the later ones. The abacus is usually carved in bas-relief with animals and ornamental flower-motifs.

So far only six well-preserved

FIGURE 3. *Asokan column—3rd century B.C.*

capitals of this period have been found, some of which are still standing intact at their original sites. Of the two discovered at Rampurva, only one is inscribed.

Asokan columns vary widely in treatment of detail, but in every example the workmanship is distinguished by precision of chiselling and a brilliant polish imparted to the finished surface. The sandstone varies in fineness, but a distinctive feature common to all Mauryan sculpture is the preference shown for a whitish stone, in contrast to the reddish sandstone which later came into favour.

In the best of the carvings, such as the well-known lion capital from Sarnath (originally marking the spot where the Buddha preached his first sermon), realistic modelling is brilliantly combined with a stylistic finish to produce a unified, organic effect, and the whole admirably fulfils its architectural purpose.

Literary evidence leaves no doubt that the Mauryan kings had many foreign contacts, and that Greeks, as well as Persians, were frequently entertained at court. This has led to the supposition that Asoka's edicts might have been modelled on the decrees of the earlier Achæmenid kings which are still to be seen on rocks at Behistan and elsewhere. The script employed by Asoka was usually *Kharoshthi*—a script of Aramaic origin, probably introduced through Persia.

The appearance of other than Indian features in the Mauryan carving, such as the honey-suckle or 'knop-and-flower' motif, has even led some writers to suggest that the work was executed by sculptors of Græco-Syrian origin, specially engaged by Asoka for the purpose. Such theories, however, are purely conjectural. Common elements in the arts of ancient India and Persia do not exclude the possibility of common sources; and it may be pointed out that Achæmenid art, like the Mauryan,

[65]

comes to us already fully matured as a composite art in which the heterogeneous influences of several different cultures are fused and blended. Neither of the two arts appears as the product of a consistent development from primitive beginnings.

K. de B. Codrington has suggested[1] that the Indian columns may have been built before the time of Asoka. In support of this possibility, he quotes an order repeated in the rock-inscriptions at Rupnath and Shasram (considered by most scholars as the earliest Asokan inscriptions): 'Edicts are to be inscribed on rocks, both here and in distant places. But wherever a stone pillar is standing they must be inscribed on that stone pillar.' Again, at the end of the seventh pillar edict, which is the last known Asokan inscription, the same order appears: 'This rescript on *Dharma* must be engraved where either stone pillars or stone slabs are (available).'

The few surviving figure-carvings which point to the co-existence of a less mature, indigenous sculptural tradition in the Mauryan period are each characteristically Indian in form as well as in dress and ornamentation. If we accept the dating of the so-called Didaganj *Yakshi* as belonging to this period, then we must reject altogether the supposition that there was no mature indigenous school of stone-carving. In conception as well as in execution, this figure suggests a long-established tradition, for which, it must be admitted, no other contemporary evidence survives.

The four examples more easily accepted as being of purely indigenous origin in the Mauryan period are the two figures from Patna, another from Parkham, and a fourth from Besnagar. Common to all these figures are an archaic stiffness and simplification of form which derive

[1] *Ancient India*, by K. de B. Codrington (1926), p. 19.

additional emphasis from their massive volume. The material employed in all four examples is grey sandstone of a type similar to that used for the Asokan capitals. The finest in execution is undoubtedly the Patna statue illustrated at Plate II, *c*. The Parkham figure (Plate II, *b*) is of comparatively crude workmanship, its rigid symmetry and the ungainly massiveness of the torso suggesting that in technique, if not chronologically, it is the earliest.

The identification of these figures and the purpose for which they were carved remain a mystery. It is not even known whether they were intended as representations of gods or mortals, although votive significance of some kind is usually assumed.

THE EARLY CLASSICAL PERIOD
(SECOND TO FIRST CENTURY B.C.)

The great sculptural achievements of this period are mainly Buddhist and include the carved railings and gateways at Bharhut and Sanchi, the stone balustrade from Bodh Gaya, and the rock-cut reliefs of the early *chaitya*-caves at Bhaja and elsewhere in Western India.

In describing the pillars and capitals of the Mauryan period, we had been concerned not with Buddhist art as such but with an imperial, 'metropolitan' art using Buddhism for political ends. To understand the essential character of the next phase—perhaps the most important formative period in the history of Indian sculpture—we must first take into account the social background and the stages of transformation through which the Buddhist religion had passed since its inception in the fifth century B.C.

It must be remembered that the religion and culture of

the Vedic Aryans had not been favourable to the growth of a monumental plastic art. The original Aryan settlers, who are believed to have infiltrated into India in successive waves during the second millennium B.C., were of a pastoral type and brought along with them a religion of abstract nature-worship which could not have taken root among a people whose social organization and outlook were more primitive. The indigenous people among whom the Aryans came to settle, living in close contact with nature and preoccupied solely with the season-to-season struggle for existence, were familiar only with a myth- and ritual-culture of the soil. Like all such cultures, it was rich in feelings for the dynamic quality of natural events and for the sensuous fullness of life—those very qualities that the Aryan priestly culture, in its development towards metaphysics and abstract speculation, tended more and more to lack.

In the Vedic period the indigenous and Aryan cultures had flourished independently, sometimes in open conflict. From the fifth century onwards, however, the social changes which gave rise to Buddhism, Jainism and numerous other heretical sects of the time, also created conditions for the fusion of the Aryan and pre-Aryan elements and for the emergence of a new composite culture. Politically, this epoch was marked by the gradual consolidation of the tribal confederations of the Vedic period into homogeneous states ruled by hereditary dynasties. In its social origins, Buddhism had arisen as a result of a schism between the two main classes within the Aryan pale: on the one hand, the Brahmins, or hereditary priest-class, and on the other, the Kshattriyas, or fighting nobility. The Brahmins were conservative in outlook and regarded the Vedas as a divine revelation, with themselves the sole interpreters; whereas the

Kshattriyas, jealous of Brahmin power and more immediately concerned with the practical social problems of the day, were ready to seek alliance with the non-Aryan sections of the population in so far as this served their political ends. Early Buddhism provided the common medium through which this alliance was expressed. It was acceptable to the Kshattriyas because, while directly challenging the pretensions of a corrupt priesthood and setting up new institutions on a wider social basis, it preserved the essentials of the traditional Aryan way of life.

Inheritance of Aryan traditions led to the renunciation, in early Buddhism, of the worldly pleasures condemned in the later Vedic scriptures. Art was no exception. 'Beauty is nothing to me,' says the author of the *Dasa Dhamma Sutta*, 'neither the beauty of the body, nor that which comes of dress. . . . Form, sound, taste, smell, touch, these intoxicate human beings: cut off the yearning inherent in them.' Thus the monks of the early Buddhist brotherhood were expressly forbidden to paint pictures on the walls of the monasteries, and the arts of music and dancing were condemned along with cock-fighting as undesirable amusements, unprofitable for the wise.

How then do we account for so much of the early Indian monumental art, nominally Buddhist, being inspired by a religious spirit manifestly opposed to the austere ideals of the early teachers? The explanation is primarily social. In opening its ranks to the non-Aryan sections of the population, the Buddhist movement prepared the way for a release of popular forces which were eventually to transform its original character as a monastic order to that of a popular religion with a cult, incorporating the beliefs, practices and modes of worship

[69]

characteristic of the traditional cults of the soil. In this
way, the worship of trees, snakes and *stupas* (originally
primitive tumuli or burial-mounds) and numerous other
non-Aryan cults, became characteristic features of
popular Buddhist worship, and at the same time a
Buddhist pantheon arose peopled by *Yakshas*, *Yakshinis*,
Nagas and other *devatas*, the godlings and fertility spirits

FIGURE 4

Outline of the Great Stupa, Sanchi. First Century B.C.

of village India.

Equally significant were the philosophic implications.
While Buddhism, in proclaiming the equality of man,
expressed a new humanism and a strong faith in the
brotherhood of man, at the same time its gospel of re-
incarnation stressed the unity of all life and the identification of man with nature. From this arose the intense
feeling for nature and animal life which we find displayed
in the Bharhut and Sanchi reliefs, where animals as well as
human beings bring flowers and other offerings in homage
to the symbol of the Buddha; in the processions headed

by gaily caparisoned elephants and horses; in the ponds
teeming with lotuses, water-fowl and fish, with here and
there a buffalo cooling itself in the water. The treatment

FIGURE 5

Mriga-jataka medallion. Bharhut stupa.
Second Century B.C.

everywhere is full of sympathy, kinship and affection, and
the theme unique, for its period, in the history of art.

There is nothing hieratic in this art, nor is there
anything spiritual. Fruit, flowers and foliage, as well as

[71]

men and beasts, are rendered with an acute delight in
their mundane existence, reflecting an attitude to life in
which any dualism between spirit and matter, or between
the mystic and the sensuous, is inconceivable.

Bharhut lies in Nagod State, mid-way between Allahabad and Jabalpur. When first excavated in 1877, its relics
had been damaged almost beyond recognition, a considerable proportion of the carved gateways and railings having
been broken up for building material.

The *stupa*, (*Figure* 4) as explained above, was the primitive tumulus or burial-mound. Adopted by Buddhism it
retained its shape as a hemisphere but became a symbol
for the last event of the Buddha's life—his achievement
of *nirvana*. Its chief purpose was to enshrine relics either
of the Buddha or of Buddhist saints, the tumulus being
built over the stone coffer in which the reliquary was
enclosed. Surrounding the whole *stupa* was a railed-in
terrace for pilgrims to walk round. Probably these railings
and their gateways at the four cardinal points were
constructed first in wood; and working in stone, the
sculptors at Bharhut and Sanchi appear to have followed
the conventional pattern of the earlier wood-work.

The scenes displayed in the Bharhut reliefs are mainly
of two kinds; the first illustrates the *jatakas* or stories of
the Buddha's previous incarnations adapted from an
earlier folk-lore; and the second portrays events in the
historical life of the Buddha, who never appears in
human form but is frequently represented by symbols
such as a vacant throne or a footprint.

Typical of the *jataka* illustrations is that of the *mriga-
jataka* medallion reproduced in *Figure* 5. Here, as
elsewhere in early Indian sculpture, the method of
'continuous narrative' is employed, incidents that in the
story occur in sequence being carved on the same panel.

FIGURE 6

The Dream of Maya Devi. Bharhut stupa.
Second Century B.C.

In the medallion reproduced, three separate episodes may be distinguished. At the bottom a stag saves the son of a merchant about to drown himself in the Ganges and is seen bringing him on his back to the river-bank. In the right upper-half the King of Benares, at the instigation of the merchant's son, is shown about to shoot the stag,

[73]

where in the story the stag, addressing the hunter king, persuades him to drop the bow. In the third episode, shown in the centre of the medallion, the king is seen making friends with the stag while the merchant's son stands at his side. The moral of this story is that the Bodhisattva (in the form of the stag), always charitable, forgives even the perfidious.

As an example of the second kind of relief-narrative, the dream of Maya Devi is reproduced in *Figure 6*. The mother of the Buddha, before giving birth, dreams that a White Elephant descends and enters her womb by the right side. In the relief she is seen asleep on her couch, with three women in attendance, one of them waving a cow-tail *chauri* to keep off flies and insects. The lamp at the foot of her couch indicates that it is night, and from above the elephant descends 'huge as a silvery mountain, possessing a radiance like the moon', as the words of one popular version record.

Among the large figures on the Bharhut pillars, whose names are inscribed in *Karoshthi* script, are *Kuvera*, guardian of the north; *Sirima*, goddess of fortune, and *Sudarsana*, guardian of still waters. Even here the conception owes nothing to hieratic canons. They are godlings of a human world whose power, one feels, does not extend far beyond the shadow of the tree to which they cling and which is their abode (Plate III, *a*). In some figures the angularity of form and the rigid stylization of dress provide a contrast to the flowing rhythm of the decorative lines on the rail copings. The work is executed with an apparent spontaneity which never sacrifices precision, and is always combined with meticulous attention to detail.

The carved gateways of the great *stupa* at Sanchi (Plate IV) are dated about the middle of the first century

FIGURE 7

The Miracle of the Buddha walking on water.
Sanchi stupa. First Century B.C.

B.C.—at least a hundred years later than Bharhut. There
is evidence that the work was not all executed at the same
time, the gateways being grouped stylistically into pairs,
with the south and north as the earliest.

Although of the same genre as Bharhut, the Sanchi
carvings show a marked sculptural advance. The increased

[75]

depth of relief, particularly on the later gateways, allows
for more variegated compositions and greater freedom of
bodily movement (the *Yakshini* figures on two of the
gates are conceived and executed completely in the
round), while at the same time increased skill is shown
in the treatment of surfaces and in the use made of light
and shade.

Some of the earlier Sanchi reliefs (*Figure 7*) are conceived and executed with the dramatic simplicity typical
of the work at Bharhut, but the subject-matter as a whole
is less intimate, more epic in character. The emphasis is
on ceremonial pageantry, the general effect being one of
movement and turmoil. The godlings reappear but have
lost their individual identity, and whereas at Bharhut
there were at least thirty *Jataka* scenes represented, at
Sanchi there are about half a dozen. In this sculpture
Buddhism is revealed in a crusading phase, the essential
quality being that of energy without introspection.

The relief reproduced in *Figure 7* illustrates the
miracle of the Buddha walking on the water. Here, as at
Bharhut, use is made of the 'continuous narrative' method
and the same technique is employed of placing all the
figures on one plane, depth being sacrificed for the sake
of a clear outline not otherwise to be achieved in low
relief. In this panel there are three episodes. First we see
three figures rowing to the rescue of the Buddha. Below,
the Buddha, represented here by the *chakrama* symbol, is
walking on the face of the water, while the same three
figures (duplicated for the second and third episodes) are
now on dry land. In the final episode they are paying
homage to the Master who is now represented by another
symbol—the vacant throne—at the right-hand bottom
corner.

The carvings on the stone balustrade from Bodh Gaya

are stylistically later than Bharhut but earlier than Sanchi. The original function of this balustrade was to enclose, not a stupa, but the promenade where the Buddha was thought to have walked after the attainment of his Great Enlightenment beneath the Bodhi tree at the same site. Thirty pieces survive. In these reliefs the narrative is more abbreviated than at Bharhut, and episodes appear here only where the posts meet the crossbeams. The carvings are, on the whole, of a more fanciful character, including in their subject-matter many of the hybrid animal-monsters thought to be of earlier 'Perso-Hellenic' origin. The Bodh Gaya reliefs are interesting historically as they appear to provide the link between Bharhut and the Mathura sculpture of the Kushan period to follow.

The rock-cut reliefs of the early *chaitya*-caves—the best-known examples being those at Bhaja in the Western Ghats—are usually thought to be roughly contemporary with Sanchi. The caves themselves, hewn out of solid rock, are full-scale reproductions of the assembly-halls formerly constructed in wood. They are the earliest examples of the tradition of rock-cutting that was later to produce the great caves and temples at Ajanta and Ellora and to play a decisive role in the development of mediæval sculpture in India. There are very few reliefs in these early *chaitya*-caves, but those we find, although less disciplined in execution, have certain stylistic affinities with the work at Bharhut.

MATHURA, GANDHARA AND AMARAVATI
(FIRST TO THIRD CENTURY A.D.)

Mathura, a great centre of sculpture during the first three centuries of the Christian era, lies fifty miles southeast of Delhi on the river Jamuna. It owed its importance and prosperity primarily to its situation at the junction of great trade routes linking the commercial centres of Gandhara Province in the north-west with Pataliputra (formerly the capital of the Mauryan Empire) in the east and the busy seaport of Bharukachchha on the west coast. Literary and archæological evidence testify to its importance as a religious and cultural centre, in which the *sethi*, or merchant class, were dominant. Within the city and its environs the remains not only of Buddhist but also of Jain *stupas* have been found, complete with carved railing and gateways, as well as many Brahmanical shrines and images.

The earlier convention, initiated by Fergusson, of classifying Indian art according to religion has often proved misleading. Indian art has never been sectarian. Fundamental differences in style, where they occur contemporaneously, are regional and cannot be explained according to differences in religious outlook. Buddhists, Jains and Hindus alike have drawn upon, and in turn contributed to, a tradition of art common to India as a whole.

The chronology of this period is a matter of dispute, but we know that it was a time of great religious and cultural ferment. The growth of Kushan political power in India coincided with the first great schism within the Buddhist movement that resulted in the establishment of the rival *Mahayana* and *Hinayana* schools, and with a widespread popular demand, common to most sects, for the use of the image in worship.

In sculpture, these changes were reflected by two innovations. The most important of them was the creation of an iconography, necessitated by the portrayal of the various Bodhisattvas and Buddhas, and of the Tirthankaras of the Jain sect. There are indications that the Jains were first in this field, and that Buddhists followed them. The standardization of the Buddhist image involved special difficulties, including that of representing the *ushnisha*, or skull-protuberance, the distinguishing mark with which every future Buddha or Bodhisattva was said to be born. This was represented at first in the form of a snail-shell and subsequently by a small mound or protuberance beneath the conventionally close-curled hair. The *mudras* or gestures usually adopted at this early period were the *abhya-mudra*, with the right hand raised level with the shoulder with open palm, to signify benediction, and the *dhyana-mudra*, where the figure is seated with hands in lap and palms open, to signify meditation.

The second innovation was a new method of relief-narrative, the separate episodes in a story being depicted in a sequence of panels, instead of within the framework of a single panel or medallion, as at Bharhut and Sanchi.

The uncertain chronology of the period makes it hard to trace the precise origin and development of these innovations. The task is made more difficult by reason of the simultaneous persistence of the traditional bas-relief style and by the incorporation of features that can be assigned indisputably to western influence.

The Mathura workshops were commercialized and served as factories for the supply of images over a very wide area in northern India, examples occurring as far to the north-west as Taxila and as far to the east as Gaya and Patna. The label 'Mathura-school' is sometimes used, but on stylistic grounds it has no justification, ignoring marked differences of style between pre-Kushan, Kushan, and post-Kushan work, all of which comes within the period at present under survey. What does distinguish all the work is the very poor quality of its

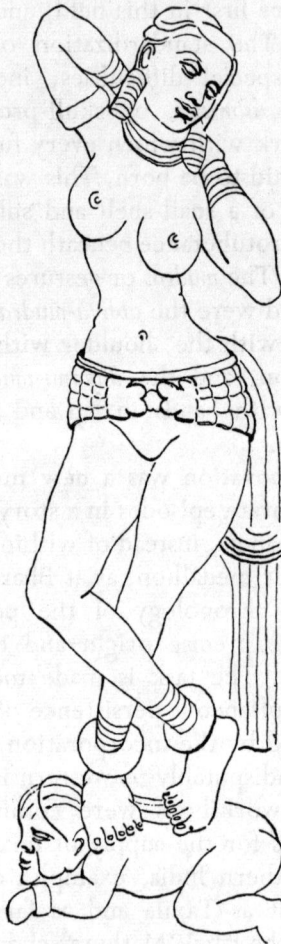

FIGURE 8

Yakshini-Mathura.   Second Century B.C.

mottled red sandstone from the Sikri quarries, the only
stone available in the locality.

[80]

In most of the carvings, particularly those associated with *stupas,* technique and vision are fundamentally Indian and directly related to the earlier *stupa* tradition. Where the affinities are most striking, however, the execution is often inferior in quality and the treatment more stereotyped. The *Yakshini* figures (*Figure* 8) portrayed on the railing-pillars at Mathura are more voluptuous than anything seen hitherto. The wide variety of

FIGURE 9   FIGURE 10

Ornamental relief. Mathura.
Second—Third Century A.D.

hybrid animals and sea-monsters carved on the medallions on the reverse sides of the pillars show a fancifulness of conception strongly reminiscent of the work at Bodh Gaya.

New qualities emerge in the designs of the deep-cut ornamental reliefs (*Figures* 9 and 10), and it is here that we also find clear traces of western influence. Eclectic variations of the Corinthian capital, the acanthus, the vine-leaf and the merman, are mixed up with such

[81]

traditional Indian motifs as the lotus and palmette. Hellenistic or Assyrian influence is also ascribed to certain pieces of figure-carving, such as the group known as 'Herakles and the Nemean Lion', and others depicting scenes of drunkenness usually classed as Bacchanalian. Even here, however, foreign influence never amounts to more than a borrowing of motives, the technique and vision remaining characteristically Indian.

Much significance has been attached to a conjecture, neither proved nor disproved, that the dates of the earliest Mathura images coincide with the first examples of the so-called Græco-Buddhist school of sculpture, associated with the province of Gandhara. With its capital at Taxila in India, Gandhara included in its territory a large part of present-day Afghanistan. For centuries past, by reason of its geographical position straddling the great trade routes between Europe and Asia, it had witnessed the confluence of numerous cultures. The term 'Græco-Buddhist' was coined on the assumption that the influence was Hellenic. There are, however, strong reasons for holding that it was Roman, and that these finds are distinct in quality and period from the Greek or Græco–Roman Harpocrates and Dionysos and the terra-cotta figurines found at Sirkap and frontier sites such as Sari-deri and Shah-ji-deri.

Gandhara sculptures vary very much in quality and have been found in the Taxila and Peshawar areas in India; and at Bamiyan, Jalalabad and Hadda in Afghanistan. Among the thousands of images so far discovered, not one of them bears a date, nor has it been possible, on considerations of style alone, to establish with certainty their chronological sequence.

The material employed in the carvings is usually a grey slate sometimes known as talchose schist. At Bamiyan, where there are remains of innumerable monasteries and caves, colossal Buddha statues have been carved *in situ* in the rock, the largest more than 150 feet in height. In the Hadda area, where stone is scarce, lime composition was used as a medium, the faces of the images being cast in moulds and the bodies plastered by the stick-and-rag technique. In Sir John Marshall's opinion, these lime compositions, which he classes separately as 'Indo-Afghan', are later; and he has pointed out that whereas the other Gandhara sculptors followed the precedent set by the early Buddhist schools of drawing on the *Jatakas* and the life-story of the Buddha for subject-matter, in the Indo-Afghan school these pictorial panels were almost entirely replaced by images.

Roman coins (*aurei*) have been found in large numbers, but so far there has been no trace of any imported piece of Roman sculpture which can be said to have served as a model for an existing Gandharan work. It is believed by some scholars that the models used were rarely, if ever, specimens of monumental sculpture, but probably the carvings or engravings on small objects imported for domestic use.

In an attempt to explain why Roman art appealed to India in this period, an interesting parallel has been drawn between the contemporary phase of religious development in Rome and the new stage through which Buddhism was passing in India. A feature common to religious developments in both countries was the popular aspiration for an ultramundane creed promising universal mercy and redemption, in contrast with the earlier and more secular traditions. In the west this new aspiration was expressed by the deification of the Emperor, and later by new trends in Christianity; in India, by the *Mahayana* doctrine with its elevation to divine status of

[83]

the Buddha who had formerly been regarded as an ordinary human being preaching an ethical doctrine. 'In the Mahayana the Buddha's birth and early life are embellished with a wealth of legendary features pertaining to his divine origin and power, which correspond to the standard motives of the Hellenistic-Roman ruler-cult. The Romance of Alexander, Virgil's prophetic Eclogue predicting the birth of the heavenly child, Suetonius's glorification of Augustus, and other Roman texts giving expression to the Imperial religion, all use the same language. The child is born of a divine father; the astrological constellation at the time of his birth is propitious; his future career is foreshadowed both before his birth and during his early years by mystical signs and miraculous happenings; he is acclaimed as the saviour inaugurating an age of peace and mercy. The parallel is so close that scholars have been tempted to establish a direct relationship between this official version of Roman emperor worship and the Buddhist stories told by Mahayana texts.'[1]

How far did Gandhara sculpture influence the development of the Buddhist and Jain image? It is a subject that continues to give rise to much controversy. Coomaraswamy's view, which is perhaps the most plausible, is that the Gandhara and Mathura types were produced simultaneously, in the middle or near the beginning of the first century A.D., and that only after the local types had been established did each influence the other.[2]

The distinctive features of the early Mathura images are prominent breasts, shaven head, and stylized folds in the drapery which invariably is moulded very closely to

[1] *The Western Aspects of Gandhara Sculpture*, by H. Buchthal (1945).
[2] *History of Indian and Indonesian Art*, by A. K. Coomaraswamy.

the flesh. The nimbus is usually plain, or scalloped only at the edge in low relief. In the Gandhara figures, with their more balanced proportions and linear treatment, the drapery hangs loosely (Plate V, *a*).

Even the briefest survey of this sculpture would be

FIGURE 11

Detail from railing. Amaravati stupa.
Second—Third Century A.D.

incomplete without mention of the standing royal figure, unfortunately headless, found at Mathura. It is identified by an inscription as being that of Kanishka, the great king of the Kushan dynasty, and is probably the earliest surviving example of portrait sculpture in India. Its harsh angular rigidity, so unlike other examples of Kushan

[85]

sculpture, suggests that it may have been the work of a Scythian craftsman schooled in India.

While the Mathura craftsmen were being patronized by the kings of the Kushan dynasty, the first of the great classical monuments of south India was being built and carved under the Andhra dynasty of the Deccan.

The Amaravati *stupa* lies on the south bank of the river Kistna in the Guntur District of Madras. Its carvings are usually assigned to the period between 150 and 250 A.D., certain sections being distinctively later than others.

FIGURE 12

Floral scroll. Amaravati stupa.
Second—Third Century A.D.

When first excavated in 1797 most of the *stupa* and its railings had been reduced to rubble and taken away as building material. Among the remaining sculptured fragments, 160 of the finest pieces were salvaged and brought to England, where they have since been in the care of the British Museum.

It is estimated that nearly 1,700 square feet of stone surface had once been carved, and this included not only railings and pillars but also stone slabs with which the lower half of the *stupa* had originally been encased. These carvings are in the bas-relief tradition of Bharhut and Bodh Gaya but incorporate some of the new features already noted in the sculptures at Mathura and Gandhara. Thus, images of the Buddha in human form appear side by side with the old symbols, and the long wavy floral scrolls on the coping (*Figure* 11) are supported by Indianized descendants of the garland-bearing Erotes of Gandharan work.

Apart from the fine rendering of flower and foliage, the main interest is in the small-scale medallions and panelled friezes which are more complex in composition than anything seen hitherto and reveal a dynamic vitality of design and a linear rhythm later to be developed but never perhaps excelled. Most of these reliefs illustrate the Buddha legend, the narrative method being borrowed from Gandharan art, probably indirectly through the example of Mathura work.

A few images carved entirely in the round have also been found in the Amaravati locality, including two fine marble statues of the Buddha, 6 feet 4 inches in height, usually thought to date half a century later than the completion of the *stupa* carvings. Here again, Gandharan influence is suggested, this time by the treatment of the drapery, which hangs in loose folds instead of being smoothly transparent according to the Mathura convention.

Amaravati sculpture is usually regarded as marking the end of the older period rather than the beginning of the new. The *stupa* is one of the last of the great monuments of the Bharhut-Sanchi tradition. Although certain of its features, such as iconographical conciseness and dynamic vitality of design, anticipate much that is in later sculpture, it has been pointed out[1] that the art of mediæval

[1] *Mediaeval Indian Sculpture*, by K. de B. Codrington (1929).

India is, in contrast, Brahmanical in essence and founded on the quite different rock-cutting technique worked out at Ajanta, Badami and Ellora.

THE GUPTA PERIOD (A.D. 300–600)

With the rise of the imperial Gupta dynasty in northern India, the mediæval period in Indian history may be said to have begun, and Indian sculpture enters a new and important phase in its development. To understand the character of this phase, some account must again be taken of the changes affecting the general course of social development.

In discussing the origins of monumental art in the early classical period (third to first century B.C.), it will be remembered that special stress was laid on the role of Buddhism and its transformation from the status of a sectarian monastic order with austere ideals to that of a popular religion, incorporating the characteristic features of primitive cults of the soil. Fundamental to this process of transformation had been an element of popular revolt against a priest-ridden social order, a protest expressed also in the Jaina cult and in other heretical movements of the time.

During the intervening centuries, this element of protest had to some extent persisted, but with unequal emphasis at different periods and in different parts of India. It can still be detected in the popular inspiration behind the work at Amaravati. At Mathura, however, in the preceding century, Buddhism and the Jaina cult were already showing signs of passing through a new stage of transformation. The growth of a prosperous trade and the patronage of popular cults by a rich merchant class coincided with the widespread aspiration for an ultramundane creed which would deliver the people from the miseries of their earthly existence and promise universal mercy and redemption. In sculpture, as explained, these changes were reflected by the introduction of the cult-image and the creation of an iconography, necessarily hieratic.

The significant point to recognize is that the heretical religious movements which had earlier represented a revolt against priestcraft were now themselves becoming established as institutional religions under hieratic domination. It was natural, moreover, that the new priesthood, drawn from social strata of Aryan descent, should foster the revival of Brahmanic traditions.

There was, therefore, a new orientation in religious and cultural life. Popular worship was now rationalized and given formal sanction by the philosophical mind, while at the same time a literary and scholastic tradition emerge, characterized by a new intellectual discipline. The Buddhist movement itself become more and more Brahmanized until it eventually lost its character as an independent movement, the Buddha himself being assimilated into the mediæval Brahmanic pantheon as an incarnation of the Hindu god Vishnu.

This process of revolt and assimilation had been fundamental to the whole development of religion in India and accounts for the exceptional complexity of Hindu mythology, with its 30,000,000 gods and goddesses, which so baffle the Western mind. First rejected, later tolerated and finally assimilated, these gods and goddesses, together with the innumerable pre-Aryan rituals and customs (such as snake-worship, river-worship and the phallic cults), survive as evidence of the insidious triumph of the popular pre-Aryan imagination over the priestly mind.

[89]

The new religious trends already present at Mathura between the first and third centuries A.D. were further developed in the Gupta period under pressure of changing economic conditions, brought about in the first place by a decline in foreign trade. With the collapse of the Roman Empire in the West, and the disintegration of the Han dynasty in China (A.D. 220), Indian trade was compelled to turn inwards, and henceforth rights over land became the main source of wealth and power. Powers of kingship were made absolute, and social relations crystallized into caste divisions based on craft-occupation.

In the sculpture of the period, the popular tradition is freely drawn upon but at the same time subjected, without loss of vitality, to the new literary and scholastic conventions. There emerges an element of refinement and clear definition which has earned for it the epithet 'classical', valid only in this particular sense.

There are two distinct yet co-existing styles in the sculpture: on the one hand, the style associated with the cult-images; and on the other, the ornamental carvings in low relief, easily distinguished by their arabesque patterns, that usually incorporate undulating creepers with large leaves curling and intertwining. These two styles merge in the carvings on the flat-roofed structural temples of the period, where image and ornament are each made to subserve the architectural design and to contribute to the general decorative scheme.

Much of the sculpture of the Gupta period was destroyed by vandalism in later times. Among the surviving images, however, there are a number of very fine Buddhas commonly held to rank with the greatest achievements in Indian sculpture (Plate V, b). These figures are mostly represented in the standing position with close-fitting, transparent robes. The halo characteristic of the period is elaborately carved with ornament and in marked contrast to the severely plain haloes of the Kushan period.

One of the great masterpieces of Gupta carving is the mutilated torso of a Bodhisattva (Plate V, c) found at Sanchi, and now in the Indian Section of the Victoria and Albert Museum. The modelling is very sensitive and the conception naturalistic. Greek influence has been suggested, but is perhaps unjustified. There appear to be closer affinities with the bracket-figures in the round, carved on the gateways of the great *stupa* at Sanchi (first century B.C.), than with any piece of sculpture in the classical or Roman style so far discovered in India.

Besides stone figures, the Gupta period produced a number of very fine Buddhas and Bodhisattvas cast in bronze and copper by the *cire-perdue* process (described in detail on pp. 54–5). One of the best-known examples is the standing Buddha from Sultanganj, now in the Birmingham Museum. This superb, reposeful figure is more than 7 feet in height and weighs nearly a ton. It was cast in two layers over an earthy cinder-like core, and appears to have been assembled in sections, one of which consisted of the head and shoulders down to the breast.

The Mauryan convention of erecting isolated columns was revived in Gupta times. The old bell-capital now reappears with bands of ornament and the addition of foliated turn-overs. In addition to capitals carved in stone there are a few cast in iron in which contemporary skill in metallurgy is again reflected. The iron pillar at Delhi, which is 23 feet 8 inches in height, is cast in one piece and weighs more than 6 tons, a technical feat unparalleled in Europe until many centuries later.

THE MEDIÆVAL ROCK-CUT TEMPLES
(SIXTH TO EIGHTH CENTURY A.D.)

It is noticeable that throughout Indian history, architecture and sculpture have followed the moving centres of political power. Hitherto, these centres had been mainly in Upper India. With the decline in foreign trade, however, and the social disorganization consequent upon the Hun invasion at the end of the fifth century, the main centres of political interest shifted southwards, where command of the routes of *inland* trade became increasingly important. In the sixth, seventh and eighth centuries the major achievements in architecture and sculpture (henceforth indivisible) owed their existence and location primarily to this development.

The great monuments of the period may be classified regionally into four main groups: Ajanta and Ellora in the Deccan; Badami further south (the Badami group being extended to include the temple buildings at Aihole and Pattadkal); and Mamallapuram on the Madras coast.

At this time the art of structural building in stone was in its infancy in India. Wood was still the material most commonly used, and the architectural features of the cave temples of the mediæval period cannot be considered apart from the wooden architecture of the royal palaces which we find reproduced in detail in the contemporary frescoes at Ajanta. There is an important difference, however, between the influence of wooden forms upon the mediæval, as opposed to the pre-mediæval, cave-architecture. The earlier sculptors had aimed at actual imitation of wooden structures in stone. Here, on the other hand, the rock-sculptor begins to work out a technique and design more appropriate to lithic forms, adapting the conventional features of wooden architecture

[92]

to these ends. The difference is clearly marked at Ajanta where side by side with the mediæval caves, there are others of the wooden-replica type dating back to the second and first centuries B.C.

The mediæval caves at Ajanta are Buddhist and were excavated at the end of the fifth and the beginning of the sixth century. They include both *viharas* or monasteries, in which the monks lived during the rainy season (the rest of the year being spent in preaching and begging expeditions); and *chaityas* or assembly-halls, designed for public use at the time of the great festivals. The style varies considerably according to date as well as function, an important development in the *vihara* being the inclusion of a shrine for private worship cut in the centre of the back wall. The *chaityas* did not originate as ecclesiastical forms but were derived from the apsidal halls used by the earlier secular communities and guilds.

The Ajanta caves of the mediæval period are renowned chiefly for their painted frescoes (Plate VI), and it is only in the later ones that we find examples of figure sculpture. The northern scarp of the Deccan into which the caves are cut overlooks the ancient northward line of communication in use during this period. It appears that after the sixth century, changes in the political boundaries gave a new importance to the Aurangabad and Ellora sections of the route, and henceforth the popularity of Ajanta as a festival centre was transferred to Ellora, sixty miles to the south-west.

Although the earliest caves at Ellora date back to A.D. 500, the most important sculpture belongs to a later period and provides a sequence to the work executed in the seventh century at Badami, the capital of the Chalukyan dynasty further south, and at Mamallapuram under the Pallavas.

Pallava sculpture of the south provides the key to the development of mediæval cave-sculpture after the seventh century. It was at this period that the Pallavas were conquered by the Chalukyas who subsequently enlisted these southern craftsmen to build their temples at Pattadkal. When, in the next century, the Chalukyas were themselves conquered by the Rashtrakuta dynasty of the north Deccan, the same tradition of craftsmanship moved further north and resulted in the creation of the great Kailasa rock-cut temple at Ellora which, in outline, is almost a duplicate of the Pattadkal temples.

The Pallava sculptures at Mamallapuram include seven monolithic shrines cut from granite boulders on the sea-shore, and a magnificent open-air bas-relief (known as 'Arjuna's Penance') carved on a slab of rock 96 feet by 43 feet and covered with the figures of deities, and human and animal life of all kinds. Two features here have an important bearing on the subsequent mediæval development: first, the type of design adopted by the Pallavas from wooden prototypes for the monolithic shrines; and secondly, the way in which the relief composition is inspired by the character of the rock itself, bringing into life and movement those qualities already contained in and suggested by the material.

At Badami under the Chalukyas, three Brahmanical caves and a single Jain cave had been excavated before the southern influence was felt. They contain some delightful bas-relief medallions and brackets related in style to the northern Gupta work and suggest a link with the earliest Brahmanical caves that now replace the Buddhist *chaitya* and *vihara* at Ellora. The megalithic temples at Badami, Aihole and Pattadkal show a line of development parallel to that of the rock-cut temples and closely linked with it, the reliefs being cut *in situ* from megalithic blocks.

[94]

The sculptors of the mediæval cave-temples were organized in guilds, each monument being the result of corporate effort. The climax of the tradition is reached at Ellora, in the carving of the eighth-century *Kailasa* temple (Plate VII, *a* and *b*). Here the sculptor departs from the previously established technique of quarrying horizontally into the hillside. Instead, he has used the narrow Indian chisel and mallet to cut through a hundred feet of virgin rock from above, leaving a solid mass of rock, sixty feet in height, from which the carving of the temple itself was begun. The interior of the temple was excavated through its doors and windows, the sculptor working from the top downwards and sideways, and the reliefs being left to the last when they were probably executed by specialized craftsmen.

A remarkable feature is the geological intuition revealed in the selection of the site to be excavated. A single flaw in the rock might have ruined the whole effect.

The *Kailasa* temple is dedicated to the god Siva and derives its name from the Sacred Mountain which, in Indian mythology, corresponds to the Greek Olympus. Here, in the restful, unchanging half-light of its rock-cut recesses, we find perfectly represented that rich symbolization of natural form and motifs which is perhaps the most outstanding single feature of mediæval Indian sculpture. Although drawn directly from nature this art is never, in the narrow imitative sense, naturalistic. The texture is not that of flesh but of stone; and the animation that seems to spring from the sculptured figures comes not from any mere linear dexterity but from energies revealed in the rock itself and the play of light upon it.

The Kailasa sculptors tried to create the effect of

movement and cut their figures in deep relief in order to achieve this end. The surrounding walls of rock, as well as the sides of the temple itself, are profusely carved with images of the popular deities, animals, and scenes from the epics; and just as Buddhism had earlier absorbed the Yakshis of the local cults, so we note here the incorporation of numerous village deities as consorts of the major gods.

There is no contradiction in the fact that this sculpture is at the same time an art conspicuous both for its conventional iconography and for its astonishing life-quality. To the mediæval Indian sculptor, no less than to his contemporary in Europe, the rules of iconography were of the utmost importance. The main point, however, is that they were important not as conventional imperatives imposed from without, but as living symbols in a community culture.

In such art, iconographical conventions are not to be confused with the *conception* of a work of art; they are no more than the *matter* of the conception. The *Kailasa* sculptors owed nothing to the iconographical literature known as the *sastras,* which belongs to a later period and was intended primarily as an aid to visualization of the gods in worship, not in sculpture.

THE MEDIÆVAL STRUCTURAL TEMPLES
(NINTH TO THIRTEENTH CENTURY A.D.)

In mediæval India, architecture and sculpture are indivisible, and it would be impossible to discuss the sculpture without reference to contemporary styles in architecture which conditioned its development.

The classification usually adopted for the great structural temples of the period is geographical and divides them into two main groups, northern and southern. This distinction is useful and perhaps necessary, although, on stylistic grounds, it is not always valid, for not only is there considerable stylistic variation within each group,

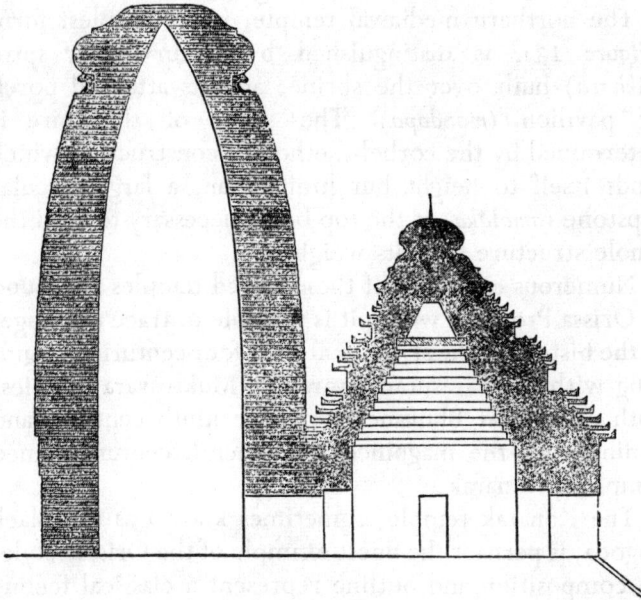

FIGURE 13

Cross-section of a mediæval temple,
Orissan style.

but in the early stages the two groups are closely related and often overlap.

In India it is not considered necessary to provide assemblies of worshippers with a roof for their heads: the aim of the temple architect is simply to give monumental dignity to a small square cell or shrine (*vimana*) where offerings are made by individual worshippers to the image or the symbol of a god. The design is conceived mainly for its external appearance, the interior usually being left severely plain with nothing to distract the worshipper in his contemplation of the image.

The northern mediæval temple, in its simplest form (*Figure 13*), is distinguished by a curvilinear spire (*sikhara*) built over the shrine, and its attached porch or pavilion (*mandapa*). The shape of the spire is determined by the corbel-method of construction which lends itself to height but limits span, a large circular capstone (*amalaka*) at the top being necessary to bind the whole structure with its weight.

Numerous examples of these spired temples are found in Orissa Province where it is possible to trace the stages in the history of the style for at least four centuries, beginning with the Parasuramesvara and Muktesvara temples, both erected at Bhuvanesvar in the ninth century, and ending with the magnificent thirteenth century ruined temple at Konarak.

The Konarak temple, sometimes known as the Black Pagoda, is perhaps the finest example of the Orissan style. Its composition and outline represent a classical feeling which, however overlaid and even annihilated by sheer exuberance of carving, underlies the whole tradition of art in mediæval India. Dedicated to the sun-god *Arka*, the Giver-of-Life, the temple is constructed to resemble a juggernaut car and to express in its sculpture the unity of all living things which derive their powers from the sun. The treatment of animal life is everywhere full of sympathy, kinship and affection, reminiscent of the spirit that inspired the early Buddhist monuments at Bharhut and Sanchi. Two examples of Konarak sculpture are illustrated at Plate VIII. The first, the figure of a musician nearly 7 feet in height, is one of a series of similar figures placed high up on the roof galleries of the pavilion. The rhythmic pose serves as a foil to the horizontal lines running across from cornice to cornice, showing how at Konarak, as elsewhere in Orissan architecture, the sculpture serves an integral function in the whole design. It makes possible that interplay between the mobile and the static which is the characteristic feature of Indian temple-architecture.

A marked feature of mediæval sculpture, and particularly of the Orissan work, is the use made of the *maithuna*, or erotic motif. At Konarak it appears in the treatment of animal as well as human couples and provides some of the loveliest compositions. This element in Hindu worship had its origin in agricultural fertility rites, especially those associated with the festivals of the spring solstice, when the strengthening of the sun was the object in view. It is an aspect of Indian religious art which baffles most westerners; yet, sexual rites in worship are by no means limited to Asiatic tradition, as even the most casual research into the records of the Ecclesiastical Courts of mediæval Europe will prove. The difference is merely that whereas in Europe the centralized authority of the Church was strong enough to resist their intrusion into orthodox worship, in India the suppression of such rites was often a task beyond the powers of the local priesthood, with the result that they had to be tolerated and eventually influenced orthodox worship.

The great Brahmanical temple constructed at Khajuraho, in Chhatarpur State, at the beginning of the eleventh century, has many features in common with the Orissan temples but belongs to a more elaborate class of design. An impressive effect of growth and organic unity is achieved by the skilful grouping of innumerable small

[99]

spires around the main spire, which focuses and unites the whole design.

Another variation in the northern style is found in the Jain temples in Rajputana and Gujerat, the finest examples being the two at Mount Abu (eleventh and thirteenth centuries). These temples are constructed entirely of white marble and are famous for the delicately carved detail on the pillars and the cusped pendants of the ceilings. It has been justly claimed that the crisp, thin, translucent, shell-like treatment of the marble surpasses anything seen elsewhere. The temples stand 4,000 feet above the plains from which the marble was quarried, and as an indication of the labour involved, it is said that the ornamentation was done not by chipping but by scraping, the masons being rewarded according to the quantity of marble dust they could show. This style persisted locally for several centuries. During the period of Muslim rule it was adapted to the decorative needs of Muhammadan architecture.

In South India, after the Pallava period (seventh century), sculpture followed a different line of development, influenced by the technique of figure-casting in bronze and copper. The influence of modelling on stone-carving was first shown in the use of high relief and eventually led to the substitution of clay figures for stone-carvings on many of the monuments.

A unique development of South Indian sculpture is found in the local Hoysala style of the Belur and Halebid temples (twelfth and thirteenth centuries) in Mysore. These temples consist of pillared pavilions (*mandapas*) built on polygonal, star-shaped plinths, and incorporate certain features of the earlier flat-roofed cave temples. The carvings, particularly at Halebid, are extraordinarily ornate and include very fine animal friezes more than 700 feet in length.

SOUTH INDIAN BRONZES
(TENTH CENTURY TO THE PRESENT DAY)

South Indian bronzes are cast by a process known as the *cire-perdue* or 'lost-wax' process, which has been practised in India from the earliest times. The subject is first modelled in clay and then coated with wax, the wax in turn being covered with a 'negative' of clay. Next, the wax is melted out and liquid metal poured into the interstice between the clay positive and the clay negative. After the metal has set, the mould is broken and the figure finally chased with a chisel and polished. There are certain obvious difficulties in this technique: for instance, the release of air imprisoned in the mould when the metal is poured into it; and, in casting larger figures, raising the mould to sufficiently high temperature to avoid cracking.

The highly specialized craftsmen who made these images were organized in guilds and known as *sthapathis*. The larger figures varying from 1 to 5 feet in height, were made for use in the great temples, and especially for carrying in the ceremonial processions at annual festivals. These images are known as *utsava murtis,* or festival deities, and are distinct from the *druva beras,* or main shrine images of a temple, which are usually carved in wood or stone, too large and heavy to be carried in processions. In addition, many small bronze images were made for worship in private houses.

The finest examples of South Indian bronze casting were made under the Chola Dynasty, between the tenth and thirteenth centuries, the best known among them being the various representations of the god Siva as *Nataraja,* or 'Lord of the Dance', one of which is illustrated at Plate IX. This theme is familiar to all

[101]

Hindus and shows Siva, usually surrounded by a halo of flames, performing his dance of regeneration at Tillai, the mythical centre of the universe. The demon he crushes beneath his feet symbolizes evil.

In the poses adopted for the bronze figures, and particularly in the treatment of arms and hands, the South Indian craftsmen have developed a highly conventionalized language of gesture. The upright pose (*samabhanga*), intended to suggest spiritual equilibrium, is usually reserved for figures of the major gods, while the female figures are invariably modelled in flexed positions, classified according to the degree of bodily sway. The commonest of the flexed poses are the *abhanga* (slightly bent), *atibhanga* (greatly bent) and *tribhanga* (thrice bent). An understanding of the symbolic significance of these poses and gestures is not, of course, necessary to æsthetic appreciation. Although the idiom is rigid, the actual modelling is marked by individual treatment, apparent if we compare separate figures of the same god in the same pose.

INDIAN
PAINTING

★

J. V. S. WILKINSON

INDIAN PAINTING

'The true beauties of art are eternal—all generations will accept them; but they wear the habit of their century.' Delacroix's remark was a wise one: garments cannot be ignored; they may even reveal more than they conceal. But the reflexion is disconcerting for anyone who would try to write intelligibly of the art of a whole sub-continent, which has worn, in its long history, such varying garments. How is it possible, in a single chapter, even if one were able to see them, to describe all sides of so many-sided a subject? Any adequate description must take account of so much else besides formal qualities. What were they aiming at, the unknown men who were painting, for 2,000 years, these widely differing works, some of them so immediate in their appeal, others so strange to unaccustomed eyes? What were they trying to express? What did they owe to patronage, to the inspiration and encouragement of great religious movements or institutions? How far were they free agents, conveying their own vision? What were their materials? How did they work? But the questions that arise are endless, and no attempt will be made here to answer more than a few of them, or to do more than indicate some of the subject's many facets.

Indian painting is a comparatively new discovery in Europe, and we owe it to a succession of pioneer interpreters, whose studies were published for the most part in the second decade of the present century, that a more general opening of eyes and stimulation of interest occurred.[1] (This, indeed, is true of Indian art generally. The bibliography in Coomaraswamy's *History of Indian and Indonesian Art* contains hardly a single entry before the opening of this century.) Rembrandt may have copied Mughal paintings, and Sir Joshua Reynolds have admired the minute portraiture in a series of mid-seventeenth-century drawings at the British Museum, but general interest was never aroused. The main reason for this is simply that Europe would not 'lift its heavy eyes and look' beyond its borders. As for this country, Ruskin and the other high priests of criticism misled people by condemning all Indian art comprehensively, without examining the evidence.[2] Ruskin himself was doubtless misled by having met with nothing but second-rate Indian sculpture.

As far as painting is concerned, several excuses can be found for Europe's blindness. To the average European, painting implies the easel picture in oils, and Indian painting, apart from the mural art, usually of a popular character, which has always been practised on the walls of temples and houses, is to be found, except for the few remaining relics of antiquity, mainly in manuscript books

[1] Not to mention many other excellent books and articles, the present writer owes a special debt to the works of Coomaraswamy, Laurence Binyon, Percy Brown, Goetz, and Stchoukine. Recent years have seen, along with a fair amount of rapturous rhetoric, a considerable enlargement of detailed knowledge conveyed in magazines and monographs.

[2] This is not quite correct as far as Ruskin is concerned. Ruskin admired the delicacy of Indian art, but thought it distorted nature. 'It either forms its composition out of meaningless fragments of colour and flowings of line; or if it represents any living creature it represents that creature in some distorted and monstrous form. To all the facts and forms of nature it wilfully and regularly opposes itself.'

and albums. The large picture intended to hang on walls is almost unknown. Moreover, it was for long the custom of collectors to keep paintings, as they are often kept to-day, bound up or otherwise, in no kind of order, and without any attempt at classification or discrimination between good and bad, old and new. Such albums can be seen in the chief public collections, at the British Museum, the India Office, and elsewhere. At the India Office, for example, is an immense collection of sixty-seven books and albums which belonged to Richard Johnson, banker to Warren Hastings. These hold a miscellaneous jumble of Indian and Persian drawings, the many fine examples being obscured by the mediocre quality of much of the rest.

Indian paintings, then, were not formerly easy to study. Another handicap (it was the same in Persia also) was the almost complete absence of art criticism by Indians themselves. It was difficult for the European to see with Indian eyes without Indian guidance. Indian painting was accordingly under-estimated and misunderstood. Indian and Persian paintings were confused, and as recently as 1912 a Continental writer, a discriminating collector and a justly esteemed critic of Asiatic art, recorded his scepticism as to the very existence of any indigenous Indian painting since the art of antiquity—any, that is, not moulded on the painting of Persia or Europe. Nowadays, matters are different. The outlines of the map are still, however, indistinct in places—it is one of the chief purposes of the Burlington House Exhibition to enable them to be drawn more clearly.

The 'Artist' (*Silpin*) in Old India was not distinguished from the craftsman. His occupation was hereditary, and he was bound by convention and formula to an extent

[107]

which limited the degree to which improvisation would be countenanced. This applied to painting as well as sculpture and the other arts and crafts. 'Genius', as Coomaraswamy remarks, was 'not an individual achievement, but the quality of the society at any given period.' Art for art's sake was unknown. The cult image dominated the artist's work, his purpose being religious and not conceived as æsthetic. How far theory and practice coincided in early times, to what degree originality had scope, where exactly folk-art diverged from that of the monasteries, and by what precise stages hieratic convention hardened, are still matters for speculation; for only scarce and scattered fragments remain to-day to bear witness to the achievements of antiquity. Certain canons of art, dating probably from the fifth century A.D. and purporting to be based on older works, prove at least that theorizing had an early beginning. They have been interpreted as the knowledge of appearances, correct observation of proportion, the action of feelings on forms, the imparting of grace, fidelity of representation, and a knowledge of correct technique.

Exalted notions of the high and saintly character required in the artist were certainly held from very early times. The conception of painting as a high mystery is not, it may be noted, yet extinct, or was not until very recently. Craftsmen trace their origin back to a divine Master. When Mr. J. C. French was travelling in the Himalayas, on one occasion, after being shown a number of pictures he was informed that no more could be inspected, as the ladies of the family worshipped the others and they could not be brought. At another time, a priest told Mr. French that he worshipped a *photograph* of a certain painting every day.

Theory apart, the Buddhist paintings of Ajanta in the

Deccan, and those of Bagh in Gwalior, the former apparently painted at various dates from the first to the seventh, and the latter in the sixth or seventh centuries, are the best testimony to the qualities of the ancient art. They are of extraordinary accomplishment and beauty, though sadly damaged. To quote the words of Sir John Marshall: 'The school which these paintings represent was the source and fountainhead from which half the art of Asia drew its inspiration, and no-one can study their rhythmic composition, their instinctive beauty of line, the majestic grace of their figures, and the boundless wealth of their decorative imagery without realizing what a far-reaching influence they exerted on the art, not of India alone and her colonies, but of every other country to which the religion of the Buddha penetrated. Nor are these paintings to be appraised only in relation to the art in Asia. They will bear comparison with the best that Europe could produce down to the time of Michelangelo. This . . . is the considered opinion of perhaps the greatest living authority on Italian fresco painting.' (Signor A. Cecconi.)

The paintings have been only partially preserved from time and the iconoclasts' assaults by the fact that they were executed on the walls of rock-hewn shrines in secluded sites far from the beaten track. Religious, as it were, by nature, and at the same time emphatically humanistic, the work of these anonymous masters impresses both by its majesty and its speaking intimacy. Much has been written about Ajanta and Bagh, and the Ajanta paintings have been reproduced in facsimile in recent years with a text by Dr. Yazdani, published by the Oxford Press.

The method of painting employed in these and in mural paintings generally, is not that of fresco but of tempera

[109]

(processes, however, seem to have varied to some extent). The rock surface was first covered with a rough coat of earth, lime and fibre, over which was spread a ground of fine plaster, on which the paintings were executed.[1]

The Ajanta paintings, executed as they were over hundreds of years, are not of equal quality like those of the scantier Bagh remains, but the best work is free, vital and varied. It is narrative in intention, illustrating, for the most part, the stories, human and divine at once, of Buddhist legend. This is an anthropocentric art, portraying the varied life of every day; the natural attitudes and postures, especially of the women, are caught with consummate artistry, but the quality of realism is subordinated to ideals of abstract beauty. In the design there is an absence of obvious symmetry and the richness of complicated linear arrangement conceals a high degree of skill in organic construction. The line is strong but subtle. The colours still retain some of their former richness. Sometimes, with a limited palette of lime, ochre and lampblack, remarkable results have been achieved.

The refined art of Ajanta and Bagh is clearly the culmination of hundreds of years of cultivation and practice. In their combination of decorative power, versatile characterization, and dramatic expressiveness, the feeling for the characteristics of animals and birds,[2] and above all in rhythmic quality, these paintings stand

---

[1] 'The technique adopted,' says Lady Harringham, 'is a bold red line-drawing on the white plaster. . . . Next comes a thinnish terra-verde monochrome showing some of the red through it; then the local colour; then a strengthening of the outlines with blacks and browns giving great decision, but also a certain flatness; last, a little shading if necessary.'

[2] The great elephant procession at Bagh, and the deer and birds at Ajanta, are particularly masterly examples of this.

alone; we do not know if they ever had close rivals. Such other murals as exist, as at Ellora and Aurangabad, of the succeeding centuries, show a weakening of inspiration testifying that by the eighth century of our era the light had already grown dim. Plate VI is a reproduction from Griffiths' copy, now at South Kensington, of a simplified and inferior, though impressive, version of the *chef d'œuvre* of Ajanta. In this famous fresco the majestic figure of the Bodhisattva, over life size, is economically drawn with rare economy, plasticity being suggested mainly by the line itself, though here, as elsewhere, there is some shading. The artist clearly has an intimate knowledge of the structure of the human form, but he has suppressed all detail unnecessary to bring out the profound pathos and divine dignity which attitude and expression convey.

Strzygowski considers that Indian art, broadly speaking, forms an island in the world's ocean of art, but that trends from central Asia affected it from time to time. The 'cube' forms in the Ajanta landscape, contrasting with the general naturalistic portrayal of human beings and animals, he regards as an 'Iranian' importation. Others have detected foreign influences from the west as well as the north, both in the human types and in the employment, though to a limited extent, of modelling and perspective. Communication between the nations of antiquity was undoubtedly far more extensive than was till recently suspected, but it is perhaps sufficient to observe here that the Indian artist—like the artists of other nations—has always borrowed from outside whatever suited his purpose.

Apart from certain early and fragmentary remains, mural work still survives in various other sites, such as at Sittanavasal (near Pudukotta) and Ellora, along with the

better-known paintings at Sigiriya and elsewhere in
Ceylon. The last-mentioned consist of representations of
three-quarter length female figures, believed to represent
the Queens of King Kasyapa (479–97 A.D.). These graceful portraits, strongly and swiftly drawn, are probably the
work of a single artist with an individual style, but have
marked affinity with some of the Ajanta paintings. In
recent years, the discovery of a certain amount of other
work has slightly increased our knowledge of the ancient
mural art in its later stages up to the tenth century.

The existing records of ancient and mediæval painting are lamentably fragmentary, but attempts have
been made to supplement the story in three ways:
from literary sources, from the analogy of sculpture, and
from archæological remains both within and outside
India proper. The third method will not be discussed
here, and only a superficial indication can be given of the
fruits yielded by the others. Literary sources, both direct
and indirect, are numerous, but not, on the whole, very
enlightening. In the Hindu epic, the *Ramayana*, mural
paintings are described, and in Buddhist literature we are
told of royal picture galleries containing carvings and
paintings. In the classical Sanskrit works, in dramas and
stories, as well as in Pali literature, painting is often
mentioned; mainly, in the dramas and novels, as a polite
secular accomplishment, and portraits especially play
an important part in some romances. Professional
painters did not, it would seem, occupy a very high
position, being classed in the *Yajurveda* with artisans and
menials. The erotic associations of the art were at one
time the object of clerical disapproval among the Buddhists, the monks being forbidden to resort to places
adorned with images, or to represent human forms on the
monastery walls, but this attitude afterwards changed

completely, pictures at a later period being credited with
an auspicious significance.

The technical literature, like all literature of the *Silpa-
sastra* type, suffers, to modern minds, from an obsession
for excessive and what often seems irrelevant codification.
These treatises were based on the practice of artists,
but they are chiefly valuable, as sources, for their
influence on subsequent art history. The manuals, like
those of some other lands, incontestably tended rather to
cramp than to stimulate initiative and development. They
are of various dates, beginning about the seventh century.
Most people find this type of literature difficult to study,
though, no doubt, much of it includes the record of
careful, if pedantically generalized, observation of long-
perished works of art. The oldest and most complete of
these treatises, the *Vishnudharmottara,* is available for
western readers in a translation by Stella Kramrisch
(Calcutta, 1924).

On the historical, as contrasted with the technical side
of painting, mediæval Indian literature is curiously
deficient, and it was not until the year 1608 that the
Tibetan Tara-natha, in a chapter of his *History of Indian
Buddhism,* attempted anything like a consecutive account
of sculpture and painting. This, though it cannot be taken
for gospel, and though it contains little detail, gives what
is probably at least a traditional account of the geographical distribution of ancient styles of painting, and
makes it clear that a close adherence to natural appearances was the general mark of the great painters of
antiquity. Moreover, by noting the different schools
which, the author mentions, evolved from their predecessors, it hints that a real continuity was to be traced
from early times. In the third century A.D., there was, it
seems, a decline, but in the fifth and sixth centuries there

was a renaissance in Magadha, the middle territory, initiated by the master painter and sculptor, Bimbasara. A western school arose, probably in Rajputana, and later a third, eastern school which flourished in Bengal, while other and less important schools developed before the tenth century in Kashmir, Nepal, Burma and southern India.

The literary evidence can be supplemented, to a limited extent, by the study of sculpture. Time has naturally spared stone where it has destroyed almost all relics of the painter's art. Moreover, it is clear from literary references that the same man was often both sculptor and painter. Only the most general conclusions can, however, be drawn from such a study; the aim and technique of the two arts being essentially different, though there is a parallelism between them.

In trying, therefore, to reconstruct in imagination the character and development of painting for the hundreds of years from which no trace of it survives, a close study of sculpture, with the aid of the literary sources, provides something at least to offset our want of precise information. At least one other art, that of the dance, is also relevant; the rhythmic principles of the dance being, in theory at least, closely interwoven with those of the representation of the human form in sculpture and painting.

The gap in our positive knowledge begins to close, if only gradually, after centuries. Of other than mural painting, almost everything before the fifteenth century has vanished utterly. The paintings on cloth have all perished. Manuscripts and separate paintings, whose life is everywhere precarious, have been perhaps more cruelly attacked in India than anywhere by the climate, the insect world, destructive wars and religious enmity. Barbarism

and ignorant carelessness, too, have played their part.
There are several recorded instances of the loss of Indian
libraries. Comparatively few out of the thousands of
manuscripts from the Emperor Akbar's great collection
still exist after less than 350 years. In India, moreover,
vellum, as being made from the skins of animals, was condemned by Indian opinion and was not used, as it was so
largely in Europe and the Near East: fragile palm leaves[1]
were the general material for manuscripts till these were
superseded by paper after the late fourteenth century. [2]

The earliest surviving miniature paintings are to be
found in a few manuscripts of the eleventh and twelfth
centuries, exemplifying the Pala art of Bengal and that of
Nepal.[3] Some of these rare manuscripts can be seen
together at Burlington House. The figure subjects are
executed both on the covers and on the narrow oblong
strips of palm leaf, held together, according to the
regular practice, by cord passing through the leaves.
In spite of this awkward form of book, the rich colours
are even now comparatively fresh. The figures are
depicted in a manner clearly harking back in the poses
and *mudras*[4] to the mural art of antiquity. Such book-
paintings though obviously severely limited by tradition
and restricted in their range and palette, are clearly the
work of trained and skilful craftsmen with considerable
command of sinuous and graceful line.

[1] Birchbark was also employed.
[2] W. Norman Brown, 'Early Vaishnava Miniature Paintings from
western India,' in *Eastern Art*, Vol. II. (Philadelphia, 1930.)
[3] Two of the Nepal manuscripts, both apparently of the eleventh
century, have been studied by Foucher, who described and illustrated
them in the Catalogue of the Brian Hodgson Collection, in Memoires
Acad. d'Inscriptions, Series 1, Tome XI. *See also* Kramrisch in
Journal of the Indian Society of Oriental Art, Vol. I, No. 2.
[4] Ritual gestures.

A different, and in many respects, unique type of pre-Mughal miniature painting, stylistically, however, akin to the remains of some Vaishnava temple ceiling paintings, is found in a considerable number of manuscripts from western India, usually called 'Jain' or 'Gujarati' manuscripts. The very individual style of these paintings was perhaps evolved under the patronage of the Jain religion, though Jainism had no specific stylistic tradition, and most, though not all, are illustrations of works devoted to Jain legends and religious biography. Secular manuscripts, however, are not unknown, such as the *Vasanta-vilasa,* a poem on spring and conjugal love,[1] and there are other 'Hindu' MSS. of similar character. All these manuscript paintings would belong to Tara-natha's western school, as the Pala-Nepal type to the eastern.

The earlier 'Jain' manuscripts are of palm leaves. The first dated example known is as early as 1127. In the palm-leaf manuscripts generally the rectangular paintings, restricted in scope and in range of colours, mostly depict divine and human figures, drawn in a curiously angular convention, and in a limited number of poses. From early in the fifteenth century, when paper had come into general use, much greater variety was introduced. The palette was enlarged, gold and other decorative devices being freely employed; and though there is much repetition of motives, the diversity of the compositions is greater than a casual glance reveals. Some Jain illustrated manuscripts are in the form of rolls and are made of cloth.

The characteristics of this curious, primitive, highly conventionalized and, as it appears to western eyes, exotic art are so many, and at the same time so conspicuous that they need not be detailed at length. The colours used are principally red and gold, with some blue. In the

[1] See N. C. Mehta, *Studies in Indian Painting,* Bombay, 1926.

human forms, the angularity of the features, the pointed noses and large projecting eyes, the broad chests and thin waists, with ultra-stylized landscapes and trees, and the peculiar methods of depicting rivers and clouds have all a decorative, perhaps originally symbolic, rather than a realistic character. The relative proportions of nature are not regarded, and the architecture is often summarily treated. The paintings are unquestionably lively and vigorous, however, and in their way the painters seldom fail to convey vigorous movement, while, in spite of a tendency to be over-symmetrical, they often succeed, as if fortuitously, in complicated compositions of great effectiveness.

Jain paintings belong, it has been thought, not precisely to folk-art but to what Mr. Mehta[1] calls a bourgeois art, developed, no doubt, from folk-art and in some ways akin to that exemplified to the present day in mural decoration. Lacking the accomplishment of 'academic' temple or aristocratic art, it is of peculiar interest, both for its intrinsic qualities and for the light it throws on the details of the world of its time, apart from the peculiar conventions accepted by a considerable proportion of the population. This painting contains clues, moreover, to the course of Indian art history. It has nothing of the grace and grandeur of the ancient art, and none of the peculiar lyric charm and emotion of later Rajput painting, with little of the realism of either, but it retains certain reminiscences of the older style, as sometimes in the drawing of animals or the 'lion'-formed male and exuberant female figures, and some of its archaic forms can be traced in the 'Rajasthani' painting into which it in fact merged—in the schematic trees, and the manner of depicting clouds and water as well as human figures.

[1] Op. cit.

[117]

The tendency towards symmetry, and the 'compartment' composition, were to reassert themselves later, and are at all periods liable to recur.

In spite of the testimony of fifteenth-century travellers as to the prevalence of temple paintings in various parts of India, there is little precise evidence of its character. There are, however, certain paintings of the latter part of the sixteenth century and rather later which are cert-ainly the product of a purely indigenous tradition, very different from, yet having features in common with the 'Jain' pictures. Even when touched, as most seventeenth-century painting was to be, by the pervasive influence of the Mughal Court style (pp. 120–38), these often have a fierce, wild vigour in the drawing and bold colouring, shared alike by examples from east India, Rajputana and the hill states, and in certain East Indian book covers. Figures in profile are stiff and ill-proportioned, trees and animals are highly stylized, water is depicted, as in the 'Jain' miniatures, in the form of series of crossing lines; while other links with the earlier work can be discerned in the angular features, the large eyes and the gestures. This is, at its most typical, a strictly two-dimensional style.

Such manuscripts as that of the *Ragmala* scenes (illustrations of musical modes) formerly belonging to Archbishop Laud, and now at the Bodleian (Bod. Or. 149) whether or not they are earlier than the beginning of the seventeenth century retain in their paintings many primitive traits, with some mixture of Mughal features. Sometimes much earlier dates have been assigned to these 'primitives' on the ground of their obvious archaisms, which, however, are to be explained more naturally by popular conservatism. The archaic element lingered till about 1700 in the Panjab hill states, owing, no doubt, to their comparative isolation from contact with the Mughal capitals, from which new ideas had long since spread to other regions. The sixteenth-century book-cover paintings of 'Mallabhum'[1] (Bankura in Bengal) have affinities with the archaic painting of western and central India, and like it, represent a survival of old tradition, which is, indeed, not yet dead, and can be seen, for instance, in the late *patua* painting of eastern India. The gods and heroes, the lovers and warriors are, like the epic figures and fairies of literature the world over, not subject to time.

Exactly how far this style, which must derive mainly from wall-painting, continues at the same time as older manuscript tradition, must remain largely a matter for conjecture. Are the architectural features, for instance, which are so prominent in the early miniatures, likely to be a mural legacy? It seems at least likely that in India, as in other countries (Persia and Armenia for instance) mural and miniature art existed together from early times, each influencing the other.

A new current, which was to have far-reaching effects on the technique and character of painting, began to flow in the thirteenth century, with the penetration of the civilization of Hindu India by a fresh cultural tradition through the Muhammadan invasions from the north. Its course is not always easy to trace, and though Kutb u'd-din Aibak's sovereignty at Delhi dates from 1206, and thenceforward one Islamic dynasty succeeded another for more than three centuries, leaving many impressive architectural memorials of their rule, no relic of the court painting of any of these earlier kings has survived.

[1] *See* Mr. J. C. French's illustrated article 'The Land of Wrestling', in *Indian Art and Letters*, Vol. I, Part I, 1927.

There is, indeed, some indication that such painting existed, though it can hardly have been systematically encouraged. One of the Taghlaq dynasty, for instance, towards the end of the fourteenth century, ordered all pictures and portraits painted on the doors and walls of his palaces to be destroyed, in obedience, clearly, to the theological prohibition ordained, though not everywhere obeyed, throughout the Islamic world. The Muhammadan conquests probably had important indirect effects, and may have contributed to the abolition of the distinction in Hindu India between aristocratic and popular art. But with the coming of the Mughal dynasty, painting-history becomes less obscure and more interesting.

Babur, the founder of the Mughal line, though of eastern Turkish blood (he was descended from Tamer-lane), had from his upbringing acquired the refined, cultivated taste of Persia. Before he saw India he had visited Herat, then the acknowledged cultural metropolis of all Islam, at the time when Bihzad, the most renowned of all Persian miniature painters, was at the height of his achievement; Babur has left, in his delightful Memoirs, a few criticisms—rather unenlight-ening, it is true—even childish, as they seem to us—of some of the Herat painters' work. Babur, however, died soon after gaining the Indian throne, and it was his son and successor, Humayun, who actually introduced Persian painting into India. The circumstances under which this occurred were shaped by the fortunes of war, for Humayun, defeated by the Afghan General of Bengal, Sher Khan, had to flee for his life, becoming an exile first in India, and later, in 1544, in Persia, where he took refuge with Tahmasp, the second Shah of the Safavi dynasty. Tahmasp (1524–76) was an amateur painter himself, and some of the most accomplished miniature work that Persia has ever known was produced at his court. Humayun was in Persia for only about a year, but in Tabriz he had come into contact with a certain 'Abd al-Samad, son of the Governor of Shiraz. 'Abd al-Samad, examples of whose work have survived, was a versatile and extremely accomplished painter,[1] fond, it would seem, of somewhat elaborate compositions, full of detail. He had a talent for animal painting and was also an expert in the esteemed art of calligraphy : one example of his skill, it is recorded, was the writing on a single poppy-seed of a chapter—a short one, it is true—of the Koran. 'Abd al-Samad was highly honoured in India, being appointed by Akbar in turn Master of the Mint and a Revenue Commissioner.

Another famous Persian painter, like 'Abd al-Samad a man of high social standing, and incidentally a poet, was Mir Sayyid 'Ali, who painted a romantically beautiful picture, introducing charming glimpses of rural life, in a Persian manuscript now in the British Museum. He, too, was awarded titles, both by Humayun and Akbar. The two painters continued to live on in India after Humayun's death, which occurred only a few months after he re-gained his Delhi throne. These two masters played a leading part in a work of great importance in the history of Mughal painting. This was the romance of Amir Hamza, a legendary history of a hero of early Islam. The project was an ambitious one, entailing an enormous number of very large illustrations on cloth, and fifty painters are said to have been employed on it under the superintendence in turn of 'Abd al-Samad and Sayyid 'Ali. This work was apparently concluded about 1575 with some fourteen hundred paintings. Akbar is said to have been particularly fond of the Hamza stories.

[1] He was called *Shirin Qalam*, 'Sweet-Brush'.

It is related that Sayyid 'Ali, worn out by the labour of superintending the work, had to perform the pilgrimage to Mecca before resuming it.

The *Hamza-nama* paintings which have survived, contain a whole gallery of Mughal art in its beginnings, though some of the paintings are considerably later than others.[1] They vary considerably in style. A few are purely Persian in drawing and colour, but the majority, to those familiar with Persian painting, are somewhat different: in fact, the non-Persian elements are altogether surprising if the superintendence of the two directors was a strict one, and if they were anxious to enforce the principles of their school. Persian painting under the early Safavis had carried elegance almost to excess; in the *Hamza* paintings there is a much more vigorous realism, both in the scenes of violent action which the episodes of the warlike stories called for, and in the representation of quieter subjects, as well as in the delineation of trees and foliage. There is less technical accomplishment: the colours are often unpleasingly strong, and designs incoherent and crowded, though there are many entrancing decorative details.

For any adequate judgment of Mughal painting, at least in its earlier phases, some acquaintance with the peculiar qualities of Persian painting is required. Generally speaking, the distinctive feature of the Persian artistic genius in all its manifestations is the blend of sumptuous splendour and civilized refinement. Persian painting is unlike any other in its application of a sure decorative sense to

---

[1] About sixty pages are at Vienna, others are in England, at the Victoria and Albert Museum, the British Museum, and in Mr. Chester Beatty's collection; others again are in America and elsewhere. A sumptuous volume, with reproductions, devoted to this work was published by H. Glück in 1925.

producing the richest possible effects procurable by subtle line and by brilliant colour patterns, made possible by costly and carefully prepared opaque pigments. 'The arrangement of colours and lines is an art,' says Ruskin, 'independent of the representation of facts, though it uses for the construction of pattern the material of life.' Persian painting, particularly from the time of Bihzad, keeps, indeed, close to natural appearances to a certain extent. Natural and significant gestures are caught with truth and subtlety; flowers and trees, the grace of birds and animals, are generally portrayed with realism. But nature is sublimated, idealized, and purified: there is in all things a suppression of angularity and obscurity. It is a two-dimensional art, shading and perspective are almost completely absent, and diversity of facial expression is seldom attempted. Sometimes, as in the frail, impossible horses, or in the golden skies and landscapes, there is a deliberate departure from nature, and the romantic purpose predominates.

For symmetry in composition, the Persian painters often show contempt. They despise the limits of the rectangular borders of their pictures, which intrude freely into the margins or the text, and as M. Stchoukine was, perhaps, the first to observe, they sometimes devise in one composition as many as three or four separate centres to which the eye is drawn in turn, uncertain where to rest. The effect, enhanced by the rapid calligraphic contour drawing, is to give an impression of freedom and spontaneity, which is foiled by the elaborate formal patterning so often introduced in the details.

It is an art full of conventions, such as the high hill backgrounds (a useful device for crowded figure compositions for instance), and certain gestures, biting of the fingers to express surprise; and it is limited in range, not only by the unquestioning acceptance of formulas endlessly repeated, but by its restriction for the most part to book illustrations of epic and romantic poems and hardly less romantic histories; but within its limits it achieved something like perfection, and it is ideally suitable for manuscript miniatures. It did not hesitate to incorporate into its conventional repertoire a few elements from the Far East, such as Chinese clouds and dragons, but it remained always *sui generis,* essentially the peculiar product of Iranian genius.

Painting in Persia, as in all Islamic countries, was a defiance of the puritan precepts of a religion which expressly forbade the depicting of living forms. On the Day of Judgment, it was held, the painter, who was the impious usurper of the Creator's functions, would be called upon to breathe life into the forms he had fashioned, and be sent to Hell for his impiety. Painting accordingly, in a world where religious orthodoxy could not be publicly flouted by the general population, could flourish only under the protection of those powerful enough to defy the ban. It was thus of necessity an aristocratic, mainly a court art, with all that that implies, limitation of the painter's freedom, the employment of fine and costly materials, and—Persian aristocrats being often fastidious in their taste—a corresponding care for the niceties of fine craftsmanship. The frown of the Faithful deprived the artist of the inspiration of a religious purpose, and probably influenced him indirectly in the direction of romantic escapism, throwing a veil of magic and fairyland over the visible world. Possibly, too, it may have been the Islamic (ultimately Semitic) horror of idolatry, that led most Persian artists to pay little attention to close portraiture; while they were content in most of their figure drawing with a calligraphic outline summary.

It was, till recently, customary to overstress the Persian element in Mughal painting, but it should not, on the other hand, be under-estimated; it was to remain for long a considerable though diminishing factor, Persian reminiscences appearing again and again in each phase of development.

Akbar, an almost exact contemporary with Queen Elizabeth, must rank with her among the greatest rulers of history. Great in many ways, he showed his greatness above all in his broad, enlightened tolerance. It was an essential part of his policy to associate the traditional leaders of Indian life in his civil and military administration. Chief among these were the Rajputs, who had come in the mediæval period to dominate and shape the culture of northern India, and to establish a tradition of warlike chivalry which has many analogies with that of Europe. Akbar and his successor chose wives from among the most powerful of this proud aristocracy, who, in their turn, played a leading part in the progressive Indianization of a court, that, nevertheless, retained its predominantly Persian character. The cities of northern India bear to this day abundant traces, notably in their architecture, of the intrusion of central Asian upon Indian elements, as well as of the reverse process. The history of Mughal and provincial painting exhibits the same interaction, the process arising directly out of the emperor's deliberate policy.

The historical and descriptive literature of the Mughal period is copious and often colourful. The elaborately detailed history of his master's life which Abu'l-Fazl, Akbar's friend and chronicler, has left to posterity is supplemented by many accounts of other Indian writers and European visitors to the court.

Akbar's interest in painting started in childhood when he was a pupil of the celebrated 'Abd al-Samad. His keen interest in and encouragement of the art seem never to have abated. He was not deterred by any religious scruple, for Akbar was so far from being an orthodox Muhammadan that his leaning towards a universal religion, to appeal to all men alike, actually induced him to abandon Islam and to found a new faith, combining the ideas of the main creeds of his subjects in a simple form. He paid earnest attention to all kinds of religious teachers, Jains, Christians and Zoroastrians. His view of painting, reverential and mystical, is clear from his well-known utterance on the subject: 'There are many that hate painting; but such men I dislike. It appears to me as if a painter had quite peculiar means of recognizing God; for a painter in sketching anything that has life, and in devising its limbs, one after the other, must come to feel that he cannot bestow individuality upon his work, and is thus forced to think of God, the giver of life, and will thus increase in knowledge.' It is perhaps surprising that the painting of Akbar's reign did not in the circumstances, as far as can be judged, take on a less secular character, but in general the worldly Persian tradition was followed.[1] Mughal art was still confined mainly to the illustration of manuscripts of Persian classics, chronicles, and tales; but besides these, Indian works, translated from the Sanskrit, were illustrated, some of them being of a religious and philosophical character. By far the greater part of the huge Imperial Library of Indian MSS. and of others executed in Persia, which

[1] Though both in Persian and Mughal art there are miniatures in which mystical feeling does find expression.

must have served as models, has perished, and hardly enough remains to trace the progress of the art during this important period with the minuteness the subject deserves. Apart from the manuscripts, a fairly large number of separate paintings, mostly portraits, are still extant. For portraiture, it is clear, Akbar had a special leaning; he himself sat for his likeness, and he ordered portraits of all the grandees of the realm to be made. An immense album was thus formed, only a few pages of which have survived. It would have been a precious record of the appearance of the great men of a great age, as well as of the formative period of a branch of art in which the Mughal painters especially excelled.

The working of Akbar's atelier is not described in detail, but it is clear that the painters were classed with other craftsmen employed, as in mediæval Europe, for the production of fine books. Members of one establishment, they were personal servants of the Emperor, receiving monthly salaries. Akbar inspected their work weekly, conferring rewards according to its excellence. We are told, moreover, that they were encouraged by a great improvement as time went on in the quality of their materials: 'The mixing of colours,' says Abu'l-Fazl, 'has especially been improved.' A few of the painters are mentioned by name, notably, besides the two Persian masters, the Hindu Daswanth, pupil of 'Abd al-Samad, son of a Kahar, or palanquin bearer, who had had a love of painting from his youth and in a short time surpassed all the others, his only rival being one Basawan (also a Hindu).[1] As well as those mentioned in the chronicle,

[1] Daswanth's name, only on miniatures in which he collaborated with others, appears many times in the Jaipur *Razm nama*, in which manuscript Basawan's name is also found. There are also separate

the names of many other 'Akbari' painters are known from the signatures on paintings; or the names may be given by a scribe. The total list adds up to nearly 150. Some of the paintings have inscriptions showing that two or more painters co-operated in the same miniature, to one being assigned, for instance, the preliminary outline, to another the colouring, and so on; or a single hand may be responsible for faces only. The system of collaboration is contrary to the usual conception of a picture as an individual creation, but in Mughal painting the individual was, it seems, required by custom to merge his identity in a common style; and, moreover, perhaps to alter his style to conform to a common manner. This chameleon quality is exemplified in another way by the evidence of paintings of certain foreign artists, such as 'Abd al-Samad himself, or Riza, a Persian painter patronized by Jahangir; both of whom seem to have modified in India the Persian style in which they had been trained.

The names of Akbar's painters have, however, some importance in proving the preponderance of Hindu over Muslim artists, less than one quarter of them being Muhammadans; while some of the Muhammadans were probably Indians, imbued with Indian ways. It is worth noting, too, that a number of the painters belonged to the lower castes, many being Ahirs (a caste associated traditionally with the cult of Krishna), as frequently appears from their names, Govardham, Gobind, Mathura, and so on. The addition of a place-name sometimes gives a clue; for instance, Kesu Gujarati; this painter must have come, with a number of others, from western India, the home of the 'Jain' paintings.

---

paintings by Basawan in several manuscripts, one in the Bodleian *Baharistan* being a noble example of his gifts.

Abu'l-Fazl pays a generous tribute to the Indian painters: 'Their pictures surpass our conception of things; few
indeed in the whole world are found equal to them.'

There is thus strong external evidence, if evidence were
needed, to prove that many of the characteristic features
of Mughal painting were contributed from India itself.
The painting of Akbar's reign taken collectively owes
much to Persia; the very conception of illustration in the
paper leaves of books in the codex form, a whole repertoire of conventions, the high hill background, the
patterning on architecture and tent hangings, and
the mixture of fact and fancy in everything—the
legacy is everywhere apparent. But from the first the
realism is closer; there are greater vigour and intensity,
a less obvious ignoring of the minutiae of nature and life,
a different manner of depicting the whole visible scene.

There was, however, a third element which contributed to the new synthetic style. Abu'l-Fazl must again
be quoted. Writing of the great painters' progress, he
remarks that their pictures 'may be placed beside the
wonderful works of the European painters who have
attained world-wide fame', and the European share in
Mughal painting, it can be maintained, was actually
greater and more permanent than that of Persia, an
influence not always fully recognized. The story of
Akbar's interest in European pictures, the effect which
it had on painting and the general esteem in which it
was held, not only by Akbar and his son and successor,[1]
but by all sections of the population, cannot here be
told in full. The subject forms one of the most
interesting chapters in Sir Edward Maclagan's scholarly
work, *The Jesuits and the Great Mogul*.

[1] Father Xavier describes how in 1608 Jahangir used to go through
his European prints with the Fathers.

When the Jesuit Mission reached Fathpur Sikri in 1580, they were told that Akbar already had in his dining-room pictures of Christ, Mary, Moses and Muhammad. They presented him with a copy of Plantyn's Bible, containing many engravings by Flemish artists; and their narratives contain numerous instances of the interest he showed in Christian pictures generally. These were constantly copied—many such copies still survive—and one of the leading Hindu painters compiled a whole album of them. Both Akbar and Jahangir adorned their various palaces with large Christian pictures. In several miniatures of Jahangir's and Shah Jahan's reigns these pictures can be clearly discerned.

Apart from direct copies and adaptations of pictures, Europe's painting strongly influenced the everyday practice of the painters. This is apparent long before the end of the sixteenth century in a greater freedom of treatment. Western schemes were unmistakably, often perhaps unconsciously, adopted in design. The miniature now admits a third dimension, and the landscape backgrounds—a new and delightful feature—are shown in perspective (though linear perspective was not completely adopted): in modelling, in the representation of drapery, in the sunset and cloud effects, in the drawing of trees and the more realistic horses and other animals,[1] the influence is perfectly clear. Real human beings, much diversified in type, and with a wide

---

[1] From very ancient times—as the Bharhut sculptures testify—Indians had plumbed the profound depths of the elephant, who has baffled the artists of all other countries. The Mughal painters especially excelled in depicting these majestic but restless creatures in all their moods and movements, and European influence only imparted closer realism to their inherited gift.

range of animated gesture, tend to supersede the puppets of the earlier pictures.

The surviving manuscripts of Akbar's time are extremely varied in character, and show a clear advance in quality from the rather crudely drawn and coloured illustrations of the earlier years to such masterly paintings of those of the Bodleian *Baharistan,* the *Hafiz* of Mr. Dyson Perrins, and Mr. Chester Beatty's *Jog-Bashist.* In the last work are several paintings of ascetics, groups of whom are often depicted at all periods, frequently with particular sympathy and skill.

With the fable books, of which several fine versions are in this country, a special type of illustration was called for, many of the pictures being of animals in their natural surroundings, and displaying that close sympathy with animal life—so manifest in all phases of Indian art—which was to appear in a rather different manner later on.

Other tasks, again, were allotted to the painters who illustrated the chronicle of the emperor's reign, Abu'l-Fazl's celebrated *Akbar-nama,* which he completed in 1602, and of which two important versions are in the Chester Beatty collection and the Victoria and Albert Museum. The subjects are, naturally, mainly scenes of court and camp, with armies on the march, sieges and battles: the emperor hunting or entertaining his guests, or gravely conversing with religious leaders, taming an elephant, or engaged in some exploit of wild daring. The artists were obviously on their mettle in these ambitious, crowded compositions. The pictures, moreover, as mere illustrations have peculiar value. The architecture of the various cities and fortresses, the costume of courtiers, attendants, and others, the equipment of the army, the furniture of palace and camp, the details of hunting and hawking—these are a few only of the many features of interest which the illustrations to the chronicle present.

The *Akbar-nama* illustrations are half-way between two traditions. While perspective, for instance, and atmospheric effects are sometimes observable (though full chiaroscuro is never introduced), they are not employed consistently; and the figures of men and women are sometimes stiff and lifeless, but sometimes alive, with expressive faces and movements. Restless surging movement, indeed, is the most distinctive feature of this series, and compensates for an uncertain sense of pattern. The colours are sometimes gay and bright, sometimes rich and sombre, but abounding in subtle contrasts.

A few words on the technique of the Mughal painters will be appropriate here, though they do not apply merely to the early Mughal period.

Paper was made in India, generally of cotton, jute, or bamboo; other paper was imported from Persia. It was carefully prepared and burnished smooth, often with an agate. In the actual execution of the miniature, the method usually employed, both by the court painters and in the provinces, seems to have been fairly uniform at all periods and was the same, *mutatis mutandis,* as that of the mural painting of antiquity. The drawing was first sketched in outline, usually in red, and corrected with lamp-black; it was then covered with a thin preparatory coat or priming of white. The outline was then retraced and the colours applied. The pigments were extracted mainly from various minerals, lapis lazuli, cinnabar, orpiment and others; but some were of vegetable origin, such as indigo or *mung*; a few, like lake or *kirmiz*,[1] from insects; the gold was from pounded gold-leaf. The pigments were tempered with gum-arabic or glue. Brushes were of

[1] Cochineal.

various qualities—the finest being from the hairs of young squirrels' tails (as, in Persia, from kittens). The whole miniature, when completed, was again burnished from the reverse side. It is unnecessary to describe the variations from the usual methods, or to detail the other processes connected with the preparation of miniatures and manuscripts, but mention should be made of the practice of copying by means of pouncings. Tracings were drawn on very thin portions of skin, the contours being pierced with small holes; these were dusted with powder, reproducing the outlines, which had to be at once drawn over. Copying by this method was an important part of the painter's training.

Under Jahangir (1605–27), son of Akbar by a Rajput princess, Mughal painting advanced to more varied and higher achievement. Apart from the emperor's revealing memoirs, there are numerous references to his fondness for painting in the accounts of the Jesuits and other Europeans. Those of Sir Thomas Roe, Ambassador to James I, are sometimes amusing as well as revealing. Illustrating Jahangir's pride in his artists' work, he tells how he asked Roe to try to identify an original European painting placed beside five copies of it made by Indians. Roe was genuinely puzzled, much to the emperor's delight, and he admitted that 'in the art of limning his painters worked miracles'.

Jahangir, it is clear, had the enthusiasm and appraising eye of a keen collector, and was delighted to receive presents of pictures, holy and profane, which Roe sent for from Europe. Jahangir prided himself on his connoisseurship, and recorded that he could distinguish at a glance the work of his different painters, even when several had collaborated. He took a personal interest in them, and tells, for instance, of how he rewarded the

Kalmuq painter, Farrukh Beg, with 2,000 rupees on the marriage of the heir to the throne. Favourite painters of his, whose work may still be seen, were Aqa Riza of Herat, and his son Abu'l-Hasan, who enjoyed particular favour and was given the title of 'The Wonder of the Age'. He was certainly a painter of exceptional quality, as were several others, examples of whose work survive, such as Muhammed Nadir of Samark and the Hindus Govardhan and Bishan Das, and others. The achievements of these artists can be paralleled only by the portraiture of the succeeding reign.

Jahangir's strange and not altogether attractive character was redeemed by his devotion to his queen, the celebrated Nur Jahan, and by a love of natural beauty which appears on many pages of his memoirs. He delighted in flowers, the names of which he loved to enumerate, and he commissioned one of the greatest of his painters, Mansur, to paint all that he could collect. His love of field sports was combined with an insatiable curiosity as to the appearance of animals and birds; these, too, were painted by Mansur and another accomplished painter of court scenes, Manohar. Numbers of these accurate and sometimes brilliant studies, faithfully drawn and coloured —a zebra, a gazelle, a hawk or scarlet turkey cock, and so on—still exist; one of the most remarkable is a chameleon belonging to His Majesty the King.

Jahangir's painters had mastered their means of expression, and had reaped the fruits of the previous reign. But one great quality of the earlier painting is now more to seek: there is far less of the stress and movement in which Akbar's painters excelled; the new and more static painting seems to reflect the spirit of a time of growing luxury in which the rougher masculine qualities of pioneers were less called for. A further Europeanization can be detected, and Western perspective is better understood. The halo appears on the heads of the emperor and religious leaders. In the markedly more harmonious structure of their pictures, the greater unity and stricter subordination of parts to a central idea, the teaching of the West is seen to have been absorbed. Shadows, however, were not employed—they were not to appear for more than 100 years, under a fresh wave of European influence, and some paintings are still close to Persian tradition. The character of the Jahangir miniature generally is mainly 'Indian', however, and we sometimes find the old Indian 'compartment' arrangement, distinct groups of figures being arranged one above the other. The delicate colours are more varied and subtly graded than before.

The developed style was ideally suited to portray crowds, and these, with the emperor often as the central figure, are among the most successful productions of the period. Jahangir is depicted in every aspect of his life—surrounded with courtiers, with the ladies of the zenana, hunting, or on an expedition. Manuscript art no longer holds the field, painting being more often employed for separate compositions. Several court albums, or portions of albums, of these separate paintings have survived, at Berlin and Teheran; another (containing also later work) has been divided between the Victoria and Albert Museum and Mr. Chester Beatty's collection. Many of these pages have borders of flowers exquisitely drawn, and coloured; other borders are filled with scenes of contemporary life, or groups, maybe, of single figures of scholars or ascetics, etc. Into some are introduced copies of European woodcuts, mostly by Flemish artists. Both in the margins and intermingled with the specimens of fine writing on the reverse sides of these pictures are many bird and animal

[135]

studies; and small, delicate figures of birds may be introduced into the marginal ornament. These are also sometimes found in books of Persian poetry, where each *ghazal* may have little bird vignettes painted with minute perfection.

Of the durbar paintings of this and succeeding reigns not many exist, and some of these are unfinished. They give a vivid impression of the pomp and circumstance of a splendid court, and of the personalities of the great men of the time. They are crowded with figures, mostly in profile, and each face is a distinct portrait. They, or sketches for them, must clearly have been drawn from the life, unlike the occasional portraits of Nur Jahan and other ladies of high rank, whose faces no painter would be allowed to see. The models for most of the portraits of women, which are fairly common, were, it is probable, courtesans.

Most of the imperial album paintings are portraits of single figures, and it is remarkable that the Indian painters did not at this time, or indeed later, abandon one peculiar convention, according to which the face and feet are shown in profile while the shoulders are turned towards the painter. This was a legacy from indigenous art.

A masterly example of portraiture exists, both in the preliminary sketch and the completed picture (the latter at the Bodleian) of the 'Dying Man'. Jahangir (who himself tells the story), with his insatiable curiosity, ordered the portrait to be made, in spite of the fact that 'Inayat Khan was obviously near his end, and the poignancy of the emaciated figure is expressed with brilliant power. This, and in quite a different manner the 'Chenar Tree' at the India Office, said to be the work of Abu'l-Hasan, represent the high-water mark of Mughal painting.

It is impossible to draw an absolute distinction between the painting of the reign of Jahangir and that of Shah Jahan (1628–58). The new emperor showed some interest in painting in his youth, and, later on, in his court library, where like his father, he often made notes in the manuscripts; some of the most famous of the painters continued to work for him; but Shah Jahan, best known to-day as the builder of the Taj Mahal, probably cared much more for architecture than for painting. Nevertheless some of the most accomplished portraits in all Mughal art, simply but sensitively drawn, almost always in profile, date from his reign; these, many of them outline drawings (sometimes the heads only are drawn), testify to the wonderful skill and psychological power of Govardhan, Muhammad Nadir, Hunhar, Bichitr, Chitarman, and others. There was a further growth apparently of genre painting, manifested in vivacious groups of servants, musicians, and the like. Night scenes seem to have become commoner at this period, as in the frequently repeated subject of hunting by night, but the painters never allowed the human figures to be obscured: they always appear as if in the full light of day, but cast no shadows. The durbar groups of Shah Jahan and his grandees, not inferior to those of the previous reign, prove that real court patronage persisted, though Shah Jahan, as an orthodox Muhammadan, was doubtless deterred from such close contact with his artists as his predecessor maintained.

Under the rigid conformist Aurangzeb (1658–1707) court painting, which had already shown symptoms that the zenith was passed, received a mortal blow. It had flourished for a hundred years. But now the imperial patronage was withdrawn, and the nobles of the court followed their ruler's example. The art could not, however, altogether disappear, though the painters seem to have suffered cruelly in status, and to have received very harsh treatment. French travellers expressly state that this was so, and that the painters were discouraged and had lost enthusiasm. A certain number of paintings of the latter part of the seventeenth century stand out amid the growing lifelessness with some marks of the old quality. Most are in the manner of the preceding reign, but weaker in grasp and execution. The best are still portraits. Among other subjects were successful scenes of every-day life and a number of dignified equestrian portraits, continuing a type introduced in Shah Jahan's reign, which was to survive in provincial art.

Aurangzeb did not, it would seem, entirely forbid portraiture, and he is oftentimes depicted, generally in old age, alone or among the troops with whom he waged his long Deccan campaign.

The eighteenth century saw the rapid dissolution of the empire. It is often doubtful which of the many so-called Mughal paintings of this time were actually produced at the centre. Many portraits of the later emperors still exist, and several of them seem to have preserved the ancestral taste for the art, but portraiture generally is less lifelike and more stylized than hitherto. Certain of the descendants of the Delhi painters remained for generations at the capital, but many sought new patrons. A local school closely akin to that of Delhi had already arisen at Hyderabad in the Deccan, supplementing the older style (p. 146). Albums of late seventeenth-century portraits of Deccani and other notables are not uncommon. These are not as a rule of high quality.

The painters, generally speaking, whatever their mis-
fortunes, were at least less tied to uniformity; their
employment, though more precarious, was more varied;
and the range and diversity of their work cannot be
disputed. It is a less aristocratic art than before, but
much of it has real grace and a new romantic charm,
though often in its subjects, portraits of dancing girls
and acrobats, scenes of comedy, love, harem life, and
debauchery, it seems to reflect the circumstances of an
era of picturesque decline. At the same time there is a
further return, in drawing, to archaic formulas, notice-
able everywhere in greater symmetry, the stereotyped
poses, the terrace architecture, and the formal gardens.

To recapitulate. The Mughal school of painting had
been fostered by three art-loving emperors, under
whom a successful synthesis of different elements had
emerged. Indian artists, their technique and palette
refined and their conceptions enriched, had rejected,
for the most part, such foreign elements as did not
suit them, and retained at the core of their art many
indigenous features, both in their free vision of life,
a distant reflection of Ajanta, and, in some of the
formulas which later convention had prescribed.
These last reasserted themselves more and more
clearly before the break-up of the empire. Then, as
already noticed, many of the artists dispersed to foreign
capitals, and diffused Mughal principles far and wide, so
that local schools, already touched with the central
current, tended to a greater conformity. A kind of
general mixed style accordingly arose, and though a
number of local variations have been classified, diverging
by distinctive qualities of their own more or less widely
from the norm, many eighteenth-century schools are
basically close together, and it is not easy for any but

a practised eye to distinguish between their products. As time went on, apart from Kashmir, Rajputana, the Hill States, and the Panjab, painters from the imperial capital penetrated not only to Lucknow and Patna, but as far south as Tanjore and Mysore, where a local school flourished up to the middle of the nineteenth century, and to the Maratha country to the west.

The chief crux in the history of Indian painting in the Mughal period concerns what is usually known, at least since it was clearly differentiated from Mughal art by Dr. Coomaraswamy, as the contemporary 'Rajput', or 'Hindu' painting—'Rajputana' in this case embracing not only Rajputana proper, but Bundelkhand, the Himalayan states of the Panjab, and the Panjab itself. Dr. Coomaraswamy, in his brilliant book,[1] emphasised the points of difference which he held to be fundamental. They may be briefly summarized. Mughal painting begins with the miniature, Rajput painting springs from mural art. Mughal art is aristocratic, refined, secular, and personal; that of the Rajputs is at once hieratic, popular and universal. Mughal painting, depending on court patronage, has its rise and fall: the character of Rajput painting, with its roots in popular religion and beliefs, is far less dependent on fashion or a patron's whim. Rajput themes are subjects closely connected with literature, often based on the national epics (especially episodes popularized in the vernaculars, that relate to the life of Krishna and his fabulous exploits —above all his bucolic sports with the milkmaids of Braj). Secular scenes are often treated; but Rajput painting is for the most part impregnated with the mysticism of such poets as Ramananda and Kabir, and with the peculiar, tender eroticism, closely associated

[1] *Rajput Painting* (1916).

with the Krishna conception, and illustrating the love, at once human and divine, of the extensive *Sringara* literature. This again was linked with the portrayal of the different types of 'heroes' and 'heroines', and the 'sentiments' (*rasa*) to which the artists gave concrete form. Other themes are the seasons, and the musical modes, which are personified; besides ballads and romances. Portraiture, of a somewhat different character from that of the Mughal painters, is also common, especially in the later periods.

Though it is generally agreed that there are marked differences between Mughal and Rajput painting, some critics think that they are not fundamental, and that Dr. Coomaraswamy over-stated his case, and gave insufficient weight to the many features the two schools have in common. They pointed out that it was prima facie unlikely that two fundamentally distinct forms of painting could have sprung up at the same time, that both exhibit the same technical traits, and that a distinction between the subjects illustrated does not establish a real duality. They further asserted that the facts of history show Rajput painting flourished chiefly in regions where Mughal influence and power especially penetrated, or, later, where Mughal painters emigrated.

Mughal painting, as an art of narrative and portraiture, is indisputably 'literary' and illustrative in purpose, and aims at expression by means of developed craftsmanship. But these characteristics need not hinder the painter's revelation of his sensibility. Rajput painting at its most typical, as in the 'primitives'[1] of Bundelkhand and

[1] The word 'primitive' should perhaps be avoided, whether we take the view that these paintings represent a partial return—influenced by the codifiers—to truly primitive pre-Ajanta forms, or regard this as an art, as Coomaraswamy calls it, of 'saturated

Basohli, is more abstract and generalized, less personal and less dependent on the minutiæ of technique, and it bears clear traces of kinship with mural art in its bold outline, so different from the Mughal painter's searching line in bright colours, and monumental character. Rajput painting is obviously close to folk art, and it did not lose this character by being cultivated mainly at the courts of the various rulers. To no one who has lived in modern Rajputana, which still preserves the ways of the past, will this fact present any difficulty, for a Rajput prince shares in and indeed embodies the traditional beliefs and tastes of the community of which he is both the head and an intimate part. In fact Rajput painting in the forms under which it is generally known, both in the plains and in the hills, remains at once a patronage and a popular art, removed from, yet akin to, the ruder handiwork of village or bazaar.

Much of the controversy—and the question has aroused plenty of controversy—about the precise relationship between Mughal and Rajput painting is beside the point if we recognize that both arts, though differing widely in extreme types and in certain developments, have much in common; that the Mughal painters, though they learned from Persia and the West, did not paint like Persians or Europeans, but like Indians; that Indian traditional ideas gained ground more and more, till the traces of borrowings became almost effaced. Rajput painting, on the other hand, while at the beginning of the Mughal period it was little affected by foreign influence, was before the end of Akbar's reign beginning

experience': a summary method of expression descended from the 'fully-inflected' classic art—a kind of shorthand not attempting detailed representation.

to assimilate the new style; while as time went on
Rajput and Mughal styles grew closer and closer together.
In the eighteenth and nineteenth centuries 'Pahari'
painting of the Hill States, again, has a quality of
graceful line, a softer colouring (within a limited
range), which differentiate it both from Rajput and
Mughal painting of the earlier types, but it is indebted,
in different ways, to both.

Only the barest indication of the somewhat complicated history of Rajput painting can be given here. As
already noted, there are comparatively few existing
examples of early indigenous art untouched by Mughal
influence; some *Ragmala* paintings reproduced in the
early plates of Coomaraswamy's book well typify the
early style; recent discoveries have widened the field.
(It is usually difficult either to date or to assign a place
of origin to such paintings with precision; some quite
late work is very archaic in appearance.) Seventeenth-
century paintings, generally showing in various degrees
traces of Mughal example—usually assigned to Jaipur in
eastern Rajputana, or to Bundelkhand (Orchha and
Datia) in central India—are much more numerous. The
Rajput rulers of these States had close relations with the
Mughal court. In the eighteenth and nineteenth centuries
the evidence is clearer. Some of the best-known examples
are the late eighteenth-century Jaipur drawings, especially of *Ragmala* subjects, and some interesting court
portraiture, painted in a more generalized, flattering
manner than in Mughal art. Jaipur work, or work of
other Rajputana painters in the Jaipur manner, of the
eighteenth and nineteenth centuries covers a wide range
of subjects of contemporary life, and is often of high
merit, especially the line drawings. This is in no sense
popular art, though Vaishnava and other themes from

[143]

the traditional Hindu repertoire are fairly well represented. Sivaistic subjects too are fairly common. The widespread artistic activity of the eighteenth century and later, however, hardly constitutes a specifically 'Rajput' renaissance.

Books on Rajput painting generally devote most of their reproductions to the art of the hills, which, with the Buddhist wall paintings and Mughal portraiture at its zenith, has probably been the form of Indian painting most admired in other countries. This 'Pahari' or 'Kangra' art, as it used to be called from the name of the state where it chiefly flourished in its heyday, differs in many ways from the painting of the plains. It has, moreover, a different history, and it reached its culmination at a later date.

This painting springs from the hill country of the west Himalayas, its area extending from Jummu in the north-west to Garhwal and beyond. It is usually classified under two groups, those of Jummu and Kangra. It has since been sub-divided into many sub-groups, the best known besides that of Kangra in the centre being those of the territories, from west to east, of Jummu, Basohli, Chamba, Kulu, and Tehri-Garhwal. The supremacy of Kangra, at any rate its lasting reputation as the centre of 'Pahari' painting, is mainly due to the dominance of all the surrounding hills by Sansar Chand Katoch, who ruled from 1775 to 1823. It was under him that Kangra painting reached its culmination, the graceful mannered drawings of his artists greatly influencing those of the tributary states of the surrounding regions.

While in its earliest phase (it is doubtful exactly how old this is), at Basohli and elsewhere, this hill painting is archaic in style and in some ways akin to pre-Mughal Rajputana work, in the middle decades of the eighteenth century this style, already perhaps affected by certain Mughal artists who had fled before Nadir Shah's invasion, received a further influx after Ahmad Shah's incursions (1761). The leading states profited, too, materially from the diversion to the hills of the trade to western and central Asia[1] resulting from the general disorder in the plains. When Sansar Chand's dominions were absorbed by Ranjit Singh, the powerful Sikh Raja of Lahore, in 1809, many of the artists whom his prosperity and enthusiasm had supported fled to other states such as Chamba and Mandi: 'The growing oppression' (to quote Goetz), 'after the death of Ranjit Singh (1839) further undermined the remaining economic foundations of artistic life. Under these rulers, the old Sansar Chand (1812–23), Charhat Singh of Chamba (1808–44), Isvarī Sen of Mandi (1788–1826), and Sudarshan Shah of Garwhal (1815–59), the vitality, chivalrous joy and mystic rapture of the high Kangra style were more and more superseded by a heavy and ornate weariness, or fashionable recklessness.' Finally, in the last sixty or seventy years of the nineteenth century, European influences, for a time resulting in a number of not un-pleasing though somewhat hybrid modifications of earlier paintings, seem to have extinguished the last traces of individuality.

Pahari art, as history and the paintings themselves make clear, owes much both to Mughal example and, later, to Europe; and it has points in common with archaic art. Yet it has distinctive qualities of its own: charm and spontaneity of drawing, an individual scale of colours, a

[1] *See* H. Goetz: 'Raja Isvari Sen of Mandi and the History of Kangra Paintings', in *Baroda State Museum Bulletin*, Vol 2, Part 1.

flow of graceful line, a playfulness and lightness found nowhere else. It is full of sympathetic glimpses of the scenery of hill and forest, and of idealized village routine. It excels in its female figures, and, like the painting of Rajputana, in the intimate portrayal of animal life. In its later manifestations it has certain marked mannerisms, its sweetness turns into sentimentality, the poses and undulating lines of the garments become stereotyped and stale. But it never entirely loses its attraction, and even in the latest work one can find examples of the old freshness and poetic impulse.

One of the few known hill painters was Mola Ram (1760–1833), to whom many paintings are attributed. His ancestor took refuge in Garhwal in the middle of the seventeenth century, where he founded a distinctive style. A few other Garhwal painters' names have been disinterred, but the art generally, at least until quite recent times, is anonymous.

Many Panjab paintings, including some vigorous portraiture, continued to be produced up to about 1850, much in the 'Hill' style—hill painters from the conquered states being employed by the Sikh rulers.

Deccani painting, already briefly alluded to, is important because in the Deccan, under the three chief Muhammadan dynasties, the local indigenous "Hindia" art traditions had direct contacts with central Asia, independent of court Mughal painting; the rulers having relations outside India, especially with Persia. Persian painters were invited to Bijapur, and several of the 'Adil-Shahi rulers especially were enthusiastic patrons of the arts. It is probable that the painting practised in the fourteenth and fifteenth centuries was largely Persian in character, but no examples have survived before the second half of the sixteenth century. In two manuscripts, one the *Nujum al-'Ulum* of Bijapur, belonging to the Chester Beatty collection, of the year 1570, and the other a contemporary Ahmadnagar MS., now at Poona, as well as in some separate miniatures of the time, there is an effective blending of Persian and indigenous elements, combining the calligraphic line and decorative features of the one with the rough vigour of the other. Something of the same quality is recognizable in a number of separate miniatures of a rather later date, with large flower forms, a distinctive treatment of drapery, unusual colour schemes and other features which, apart from the details of costume and the profusion of jewellery, differentiate them from contemporary Mughal painting. Miss Stella Kramrisch[1] reproduces some interesting wall paintings from the Water Pavilion of Kumatgi, Bijapur, with close resemblances to these miniatures.

The earlier manuscript paintings mentioned above, and a *Rag-mala* miniature[2] in the Baroda Museum, seem to illustrate a powerful Hindu infiltration which followed close on the collapse after 1565 of Vijayanagar, and the dispersal of its painters, with other artists of a splendid court, to the southern Muslim capitals. They seem to presage a mingling of styles which more than a century later characterized Indian painting generally.

Under Jahangir and Shah Jahan there was fairly close relationship between the Mughal and Deccani rulers, and it is possible that Mir Hashim, who painted several Deccani portraits and became one of the most accomplished portraitists at the Mughal Court, may have

[1] 'A Survey of Painting in the Deccan' (India Society, 1937).
[2] Described and reproduced by Dr. Goetz in the *Baroda State Museum Bulletin*, Vol. I, No. 1.

originally come from the Deccan. Some Golconda paintings of the latter half of the seventeenth century in the Sir Akbar Hydari collection and elsewhere, both of provincial scenes and of single figures, have considerable power and a certain monumental quality which distinguish them from the usual run of rather indifferent portraiture.

One or two examples of the delicate work of a Deccani painter named Rahim,[1] apparently of the end of the seventeenth century, exemplify a transient phase of *fin-de-siècle* originality. It is interesting to trace the different elements from north, south, and west, in their eclecticism.

Some celebrated painters and miniaturists from Europe, Zoffany, Smart, and others, worked in India towards the end of the eighteenth century. Though very little direct imitation of their work is traceable in that of the Indian artists, they must have contributed to the increasing European vogue. Indian painters, working in a bastard style, were often employed to make portraits of British civil and military officers. These, often of great historical interest, at times show that the old gift for portraiture was not yet extinguished. Oil paintings were commissioned by the Oudh rulers[2] and other potentates, to the further detriment of indigenous talent, which had for the most part, with the exception of some moderately competent painting at Patna and elsewhere, rather lost its way.

Early in the twentieth century there was a deliberate attempt, fostered by the late Abanindranath Tagore,

[1] See Plate XIV, and Kramrisch, *op. cit.*, Plate XXI.
[2] It is exceptional to find in Lucknow painting, often garish and pretentious, any real merit.

Mr. E. B. Havell and others, to bring about a national renaissance, with the aid of the study of masterpieces, first those of India's past, from Ajanta to the Mughal and 'Pahari' miniatures, and, later, Chinese and Japanese paintings. The stimulus was an artificial one, and, of course with exceptions, resulted in rather weak and mannered productions, without disclosing any great individual genius; but the movement did a real service in awakening a general interest in the theory and practice of painting. Schools of Art were established in many parts of India, and technical training was encouraged.

To-day, currents from many directions are flowing in the Indian art world, that from France being probably the strongest. There is certainly a new awakening and, among other developments, there are signs of the growth of a purely landscape art—a new thing in India; but it is difficult at present to forecast the outcome of the present stage of restless exploration. Generally speaking, Indians in many quarters, while aware of their own varied artistic heritage, have by no means closed their eyes to the technique and experience of the West. At the same time, it is significant that some of the most respected figures in the contemporary world are paying more attention to the still living, timeless folk-art of the villages, which has never been extinguished.

There are many ways of regarding the painting of India. It may, for instance, be viewed as a vast tract, much of it more or less obscure, out of which scattered points appear more distinctly—Ajanta, Delhi, or the Himalayas —distinct but independent, each to be appraised and admired by itself. We may again view its whole extent, and try to follow its evolution, to seize its general character, and to estimate the nature and value of its revelation. We can analyse its origins and its different components, and separate its styles, distinguishing the academic or hieratic from the popular, the polished art of courts or wealthy institutions from that of the people, the foreign from the indigenous elements. Various aspects, æsthetic, sociological, and so on, appeal to different minds; or, again, painting may be scanned for its value as an adjunct to history—with its varied portraiture of past ages and its records of the architecture, costume, and apparatus of everyday life. In whichever way it is approached, it will reward attention and study. Indian painting is rich and varied enough to yield profit and delight to every taste, and it has the additional attraction that many of its problems still await solution.

THE MINOR ARTS
OF INDIA

★

K. DE B. CODRINGTON

THE MINOR ARTS OF INDIA

1. ART AND INDUSTRY OF INDIA

It is customary to speak of India as a sub-continent and, in view of her size, to stress the complexity of her culture. This is largely due to preoccupation with the present Hindu-Muslim political conflict, a preoccupation that may be corrected by remembering that China also is very big and has a large Muslim population and yet is commonly regarded as the supreme example of cultural unity. History, too, does not support the idea of an essentially divided India. At many periods there has been no Muslim problem in Hindu India and no Hindu problem in Muslim India, and throughout the centuries, since Kutbu'd-din employed Hindu masons to raise up his great Strength of Islam Mosque upon the ruins of Hindu Delhi, there has been a free exchange of services and goods from the centres of the population of the one faith to the centres of the other. All over the world, cities tend to be complex and even polyglot. In spite of industrialization, India remains a land of villages and it is in the villages, whether of the Hindu areas or the Muslim areas, that the true basis of Indian culture must be sought. The plough and the harrow and the seed-drill used in southern Madras are the same as those used in the Panjab; the potter's wheel, the spinning-wheel and the weaver's loom are the same, and so is the women's jewellery. In spite of the multiplicity of languages, the very turn of phrase of the proverbs, which are the poetry of village speech, is identical, as are the songs of the countryside, both words and music; all of which must be set against the same

[153]

background of the changing seasons from seed-time to harvest, dominated by the vital importance of rainfall. It is not for nothing that, all over India, the well or tank is the focus of the social life of the villages, the meeting place of the past and present, where, in the deliberation of the elders and the talk of the women as they draw the water for the evening meal, the India of the future is being built day by day; where the children play the games Indian children always have played and the cattle come down to water as they always have done. The subject is worthy of poetry but, as a corrective to the merely senti-mental, the bucket swinging at the well-head is factory made and there are many roofs in the village of corrugated iron and in the village square there is a gaily painted motor-bus, one of the thousands which, bumping and rattling across the dusty roads of India, have given the country a new unity.

As in the West, much of the colour of life has gone from the cities, but beyond them, especially on the little roads that link village with village and the fields between, the old colours and patterns persist. Passing through the sun-stricken hot-weather countryside, it is still notice-able how prominent man and his personal effects are in the landscape. The varied Indian scene is, at all seasons, beautiful in itself. Its variety is the frame and mould of India's richly variegated life. Here individuality does not degenerate into eccentricity, but is schooled by a social unity such as cities cannot know. The traditional is not to be confused with the archaic, or merely effete, but has a dignity and value of its own, springing from the very origins of society. As everywhere, the countryside in India has remained simpler than the town, not merely in organization or technically, but in manner. Its life, how-ever, is not static. The changing shows and fashions of the cities catch the eye more easily and follow each other more quickly. Change here is slower and more akin to growth. To those that have eyes to see, history is made visible in the very designs of the women's *saris* and the forms of the pots they carry down to the water. The pattern of the heavy silver anklets of the well-to-do farmer's wife persists among out-of-the-way forest tribes, who belong to India's most ancient past. The bold, flowered print of the woman of the Lamani bullock-carrier people is historic, for it bears witness to the courtly interest in Persian fashions in the seventeenth century, when the Safavid and Mughal empires were at their greatest. Tobacco, which is universal, and red

FIGURE 14.   *Silver Bangle. Deccan.*

peppers, without which it is difficult to imagine Indian food, belong to the New World and are recent in India, hardly less recent than the Victorian-Gothic of the Victoria terminus at Bombay or the conscientiously Indianized architecture of New Delhi. There is only this distinction: that the villages absorb and preserve that for which they have a use while the cities are full of out-worn cultural mausolea. The culture of a society is not its art or industry, commerce or politics, but what endures as against the passing show of fashion.

[155]

There are some who will say that the Fine Arts of India, that is to say, sculpture and painting, are dead. It is not true, for the Art Schools are full and much work is being done. All that can justly be said is that the sculpture and painting of modern India are of to-day. It is right that it should be so, for in these things there can be no turning back. The use of the term Industrial Art, on the other hand, does not fit in with the Indian picture at all. All over India, distinctive kinds of embroidery are done by the women of different castes or classes, and there are many other crafts which spring from the home or the village, and belong to it and not to industry, as the West knows it. In the industrial development of the West, between the modern mass-production factory and the old home crafts, came the home factory where the master worked, surrounded by his paid workmen and apprentices. In India, it is still possible to see the master-weaver sitting at his simple loom at the street corner, where in spring the scarlet blossoms of the gold mohurs fall upon the web as it is born beneath hands schooled by generations of skilled work. The mills of Ahmedabad and Bombay, the Tata steel-works and the Bengal collieries are salient features of the India of to-day, as the projected hydro-electric works will doubtless be of the India of to-morrow. But, in contradistinction to the West, all this centralization has not quite submerged the older tradition of personal skill and personal pride in a living tradition. Interest in arts and crafts in the West exists largely as a reaction from mechanization and the mechanized nature of modern life. In India it still survives in its own right, though localized and diminished in scope and possibly doomed to die, as our own native crafts have died in the West.

2. THE ARTIST AND THE PATRON

A satisfactory definition of art still eludes the critic. As an activity, art is, of course, a form of expression. All great art implies a statement, the painter using his coloured earths and the sculptor the natural stone, as poets use words. In all these cases, however, the statement is not merely one of fact. The speech of everyday life is not poetry, for the poet evidently brings to his work a certain skill not given to ordinary men. The critic, who writes about art, is usually wanting in the very particular ability given to artists, which is to show that the essential quality of art lies in the doing. It was the critic who postulated 'pure form' and 'tactile imagination' and 'the architectonic' and 'the functional' and all the other clichés of the trade. The fact remains that painting and sculpture exist and that they have a strange power of attraction over the mind of mankind. It is common knowledge that the personality of the artist is implicated in his work, and that he must be reckoned with as an individual. The artist is assuredly his style. Moreover, to the historian who has his own special interests in periods and the waxing and waning of significant human activity, the artist belongs to his time and must be looked at against the known facts of the political and material background. If the theories of the critic are reviewed historically, it will be seen that criticism has its periods too, as well as art. At one time, naturalism has been the reigning interest, at another, literary sentiment. Later, technical proficiency comes into the foreground, and later still, formal values which have nothing to do with naturalism or literature, and little connection with technique. In this last stage, it is possible that the artist tends to lose himself in the critic and his special

[157]

gift of action to be submerged in theory. To-day it is possible that the pendulum has already begun to swing away from the doctrinaire towards a simpler appreciation of human interests and a less doctrinaire approach to art. The gravity of the problems that weigh upon us makes it inevitable that we should turn again to tradition with renewed seriousness, partly as a relief from present necessities, partly in the hope of unravelling the secret of the great decades of achievement, from which we derive our cultural heritage.

The periodic or cataclysmic view of history is not altogether justified. The glory of Greece is no more and Rome has shrunk to the few acres of the Papal State. The ancient empires of the East have vanished utterly. But, in point of fact, in China and in India, the ancient tradition lives and has never been broken. In discussing any of the arts, it is always necessary to pay attention to tradition. As against the post-Renaissance view of the artist as genius, it is necessary to consider him as craftsman. Even in the Fine Arts, originality is not the only secret of great art; for though a genius may influence his generation and the future, he is of his time and son of his father. Before apprenticeship in the Renaissance studios became the vehicle of tradition, the mediæval craftsmen had their guilds; India, too, had its own system of ancient craft- and trade-guilds. But apart from this, apart from the educational functions of the organization of the crafts, tradition is inherent in art of all kinds. The artist lives in his eyes; the child sees what there is to see. The centuries take their toll of the monuments of the past and the remnant, as we find it, is not necessarily representative. The dogmatic identification of art with religion may well be challenged, though all over the world, religious buildings, paintings and sculpture survive, where the houses of common men, including kings, have vanished. In India, especially, the custom of pilgrimage has always linked the past with the present indissolubly. Beyond the walls of the official seat of the new Government of India in New Delhi, lie the ruins of its seven predecessors, providing a record of over a thousand years of Indian architectural development.

Just as the problem of art cannot be confined to the artist's genius, it is also necessary to go beyond his personal vision. Man does not live by bread alone, but he cannot live without it. We know that Pisanello saw Fra Angelico's 'Crucifixion' in St. Mark's Chapter House, for his sketches of it still exist. His interest in land-scape and his love of bright colours may be said to be his own, but it is undoubtedly true that it was the taste of his princely patrons that moulded the form of his art and made it possible. It was the patronage of the princely houses of the Italian cities that created Renaissance art, just as it was the patronage of the great ecclesiastical foundations which made Gothic architec-ture and sculpture possible. The patronage of the earlier period was necessarily restricted in kind. The essence of the Renaissance was a breaking down of artistic limita-tions, an enlargement of opportunity, always, of course, at the wish of the patron. So it is that the painter-client turned his hand to bridal chests and majolica dinner services, and, in the case of Raphael and others, to stage-settings, and, in the case of Leonardo, to making a garden-house and a bath for Beatrice d'Este. The patron's whim must be fulfilled, but by this association with the great the artist won gentility, though the price paid for it included the seeds of the drapery-hanging and phiz-mongering, which Hogarth so rightly fulminated against. Henceforward, in the West, the arts were divided into two distinct categories, the Fine Arts of the gentlemen painters and sculptors, and the Mechanic or Industrial Arts.

The distinction is real to a certain extent, for with the rise of the new commercial plutocracy in the seventeenth century there came into being a general demand for fine furniture, hangings, glass and silverware, a demand which was inspired and dominated by the fashions set by the courts and noble houses of Europe. This widespread demand could only be satisfied locally and, in most cases, the local craftsman was incapable of turning out the looked-for fashionable designs. Daniel Marot and others responded to the need by publishing engraved designs for the necessary articles, ranging from coaches to cutlery. Chippendale's 'Directory' fulfilled the same need and the wide range of country Chippendale furniture demonstrates the process in detail. Based on the master's designs, the specimens vary from conscientious journeyman copies to palpable misunderstandings. The process is continued through the trade-journals to the present day.

In India, an identical process of patronage may be observed, for the Mughal emperors were great patrons of the arts. They looked to Safavid Persia for their models and, as in Europe, court fashions spread through the nobility to the provinces. Sir John Chardin in his *Journal du Voyage*[1] describes the workshop (*Carconés*) of the Persian king and his courtly followers, which he compares with the galleries of the Louvre and the palace of the Grand Duke of Florence. He says that large numbers of hereditary master-workmen were employed in these workshops on a regular salary with rations. They were provided with all the materials necessary, and received a reward and an increase of salary for every masterpiece they produced. In the same way, the great Mughal emperors,

[1] 1664-70.

Akbar, Jahangir and Shah Jahan, maintained skilled work-men of all kinds at their courts. Abu'l-Fazl, in his *Institutes of Akbar,* the official record of the organization and routine of the court, describes the various crafts which received the royal patronage. Akbar was interested not merely in painting. He found time to give his personal attention to the royal armoury and to the forging and decorating of the weapons made there. In the royal wardrobe were to be found the products of all nations, carefully preserved for the emperor's use, or to give away as presents to favoured courtiers or guests. At his command, many new crafts were established at the imperial capital. The skill of the weavers and embroiderers of Delhi was such that the finest products of Persia, China and Europe were eclipsed and found no sale. Abu'l-Fazl speaks of jewellers, engrav-ers of precious stones, inlayers of gold, damascene-workers, enamellers, filigree-workers, makers of gold and silver lace, and workers in crystal and carnelian. This list is corroborated by many travellers. Terry, in his *Voyage to the East Indies,*[1] writes: 'The natives there shew very much ingenuity in their curious manufactures, as in their silk stuffs, which they most artificially weave, some of them very neatly mingled either with silver or gold, or both, as also in making excellent quilts of their stained cloth, or of fresh-coloured taffeta lined with their pinta-does (painted fabrics), or of their satin lined with taffeta, betwixt which they put cotton wool, and work them together with silk. . . . They make likewise excellent carpets of their cotton wool, in mingled colours, some of them three yards broad and of a great length. Some other richer carpets they make all of silk, so artificially mixed as that they lively represent those flowers and figures made in them. The ground of some others of their very

[1] 1655.

rich carpets is silver or gold, about which are such silken flowers and figures most excellently and orderly disposed throughout the whole work. Their skill is likewise exquisite in making of cabinets, boxes, trunks and standishes, curiously wrought within and without; inlaid with elephants' teeth or mother-of-pearl, ebony, tortoiseshell, or wire. They make excellent cups and other things of agate or carnelian, and curious they are in cutting of all manner of stones, diamonds as well as others. They paint staves or bedsteads, chests or boxes, fruit dishes or large chargers extremely neat, which, when they be not inlaid as before, they cover the wood, first being handsomely turned, with a thick gum, then put their paint on most artificially made of liquid silver or gold or other lively colours which they use, and after make it much more beautiful with a very clear varnish put upon it. They are also excellent at limning, and will copy out any picture they see to the life. . . . The truth is, that the natives of that monarchy are the best apes for imitation in the world, so full of ingenuity that they will make any new thing by pattern, how hard soever it seem to be done, and therefore it is no marvel if the natives there make boots, cloths, linen, bands, cuffs of our English fashion, which are all very much different from their fashions and habits, and yet make them all exceedingly neat.'

But such accounts deal with the passing glories of the courts of Akbar, Jahangir and Shah Jahan. Already under Aurangzeb, the flower had perished and the glory departed. Opinions may differ as to the absolute beauty of the Taj Mahal, but it is the masterpiece of its age, unsurpassed in its kind, indeed, unchallenged. Tavernier,[1] who was there, says that it took twenty thousand labourers twenty-two years to build it and that the brick scaffolding

[1] *Travels*, Vol. I, p. 110.

cost as much as the building itself. Under Aurangzeb, after the imprisonment of the old Emperor and the murder of Dara Shikoh, such things were no longer possible. Aurangzeb was not merely a Muslim bigot; many devout Muslims have been patrons of the arts. But political ruthlessness and dogmatic orthodoxy are certainly no substitute for personal interest where the arts are concerned. Aurangzeb was, however, a realist. He may have seen that the era was finished and could not be protracted. In a country where the margin between subsistence and starvation is so narrow, the cost of public works, artistic or otherwise, must be considered. History makes it clear that under certain conditions art costs too much. It is not merely a matter of the willingness of the patron to pay; Aurangzeb did not merely neglect the arts. The truth is that the system, which made that kind of patronage, and that kind of art, possible, had bled the country white. It is the patron that costs too much, not the artist.

Bernier was a good economist and in his *Letters to Colbert*[1] he analyses the naked and ugly facts that lay behind the dying splendours of the Mughal empire. He writes: 'The persons . . . in possession of the land . . . have an authority almost absolute over the peasantry, and nearly as much over the artisans and merchants of the towns and villages within their district; and nothing can be imagined more cruel and oppressive than the manner in which it is exercised. . . . This debasing state of slavery obstructs the progress of trade and influences the manners and mode of life of every individual. There can be little encouragement to engage in commercial pursuits, when the success with which they may be attended, instead of adding to the enjoyments of life, provokes the cupidity of a neighbouring tyrant possessing both power and inclination

[1] 1656-68.

to deprive any man of the fruits of his industry. . . .
It is owing to this miserable system of government that
most towns in Hindoustan are made up of earth, mud and
other wretched materials; that there is no city or town
which, if it be not already ruined and deserted, does not
bear evident marks of approaching decay. . . . Can it
excite wonder, that under these circumstances, the arts
do not flourish here as they would do under a better
government, or as they flourish in our happier France? No
artist can be expected to give his mind to his calling in the
midst of a people who are either wretchedly poor, or
who, if rich, assume an appearance of poverty, and who
regard not the beauty and excellence, but the cheapness of
an article: a people whose grandees pay for a work of art
considerably under its value and according to their own
caprice and who do not hesitate to punish an importunate
artist, or tradesman, with the *korrah,* that long and terrible
whip hanging at every *Omrah's* gate. Is it not enough also
to damp the ardour of any artist, when he feels that he can
never hope to attain to any distinction; that he shall not
be permitted to purchase either office or land for the
benefit of himself and family; that he must at no time
make it appear he is the owner of the most trifling sum;
and that he may never venture to indulge in good fare, or
to dress in fine apparel, lest he should create a suspicion
of his possessing money. The arts in the Indies would
long ago have lost their beauty and delicacy if the
Monarch and principal *Omrahs* did not keep in their pay
a number of artists who work in their houses, teach the
children, and are stimulated to exertion by the hope of
reward and the fear of the *korrah.* The protection
afforded by powerful patrons to rich merchants and
tradesmen who pay the workmen rather higher wages,
tends also to preserve the arts. I say rather higher wages,

for it should not be inferred from the goodness of the manufactures, that the workman is held in esteem, or arrives at a state of independence. Nothing but sheer necessity or blows from a cudgel keep him employed; he can never become rich, and he feels it no trifling matter if he have the means of satisfying the cravings of hunger and of covering his body with the coarsest raiment. . . . The country is ruined by the necessity of defraying the enormous charges required to maintain the splendour of a numerous court, and to pay a large army maintained for the purpose of keeping the people in subjection. . . .'

3. EVERYDAY ART

It is plain then, that the facts that lie behind Mughal magnificence correspond very closely with those that underlay the development of the arts in Renaissance Italy. The Fine Arts, as they then existed, were not merely non-industrial or un-commercial. In the West, the painter and sculptor managed to win a degree of preferential treatment for themselves; in England these ambitions were confirmed by the foundation of the Royal Academy and the knighting of its presidents. But this social symbolism was actually the manifestation of far more radical changes. The anonymity of the Middle Ages was dead and the artists lived and worked in person. So radical was the new cult of personality that until quite recently the history of art has been little more than anecdotes of artists. From it inevitably sprang the cult of originality, to which the patrons readily responded, for the dilettante has always found it easy to admire the new and the strange. The fashionable, however, is only available to those that can afford it. The art of the patron is essentially an art of fashions.

[165]

In 1880, Birdwood published his *Industrial Art of India* as a handbook to 'the important collection of examples comprised in the Museum originally formed by the East India Company . . . lately transferred from the India Office . . . to the South Kensington Museum'. It is intelligible that a trading company should wish to have a collection of the arts of the country it traded with. Future historians may wonder why the India Office should be willing to do without it, and what the consequences of this were. Birdwood had no mind for the Fine Arts, but he loved handicraft and the colour and movement of the Indian scene. In Ruskinian vein, he claimed fine artistry for the weavers, potters and coppersmiths of India. This very sincere admiration is sometimes a little inconsequent, for instance, where he writes: 'In India everything is hand wrought and everything, down to the cheapest tools or earthen vessel, is therefore more or less a work of art.' He regrets the immediate results of the impingement of West upon East: 'Indian collections are now . . . to be seen to be more and more overcrowded with mongrel articles, the result of the influences on Indian art of European society, European education, and above all of the irresistible energy of the mechanical productiveness of Birmingham and Manchester. . . . The worst mischief is perhaps done by the architecture foisted on the country by the Government of India, which being the architecture of the State is naturally thought to be worthy of imitation. . . . Through all these means, foreign decorative forms are being constantly introduced and foreign fashions set; and so rapidly are they spreading that there is a real fear that they may at last irretrievably vitiate the native tradition of the distinctive arts of India. . . .' In 1880, he was able to write: 'The social and moral evils of the introduction of machinery into India are likely to be still

[166]

greater. At present, the industries of India are carried on all over the country, although hand-weaving is everywhere languishing in the unequal competition with Manchester and the Presidency Mills. But in every Indian village the traditional handicrafts are still to be found at work.'

This is now only partially true. The bulk of the Jaipur workshops are devoted to the tourist-trade, though the perennial Indian interest in jewellery has at least preserved the standards of that ancient craft. At Aurangabad in H.E.H. the Nizam's dominions, a few looms, aided by a state subsidy, still produce their once famous *mashru* brocades, which find a sparse market among Muhammadans as wedding-coats. Here, as with the Jaipur jewellery, the craft is based upon a social need and will survive as long as that need survives. Jewellery, however, is intrinsically valuable; indeed in India, as during financial depressions in the West, it becomes a kind of currency. A brocaded coat, however fitting for a marriage, has no essential value and there is a limit to what people are willing, or able, to pay for it. The weavers of Aurangabad are using artificial silk in order to keep their prices down and maintain their market. The end is within sight and another fragment of the past will surely die. It will die because it has become too expensive, not because the work has deteriorated, or because of the competition of the machine and the wholesaler.

Birdwood writes lovingly of the old crafts of India, and his picture of the Indian market-town, as it once was, is not exaggerated: 'Outside the entrance, on an exposed rise of ground, the hereditary potter sits by his wheel moulding the swift revolving clay by the natural curves of his hands. At the back of the houses, which form the low irregular street, there are two or three looms at work in blue and scarlet and gold. . . . In the street the brass- and

[167]

copper-smiths are hammering away at their pots and pans; and further down, in the verandah of the rich man's house, is the jeweller working rupees and gold mohurs into fair jewellery, gold and silver earrings, and round tires like the moon, bracelets and tablets and nose rings, and tinkling ornaments for the feet, taking his designs from the fruits and flowers around him, or from the traditional forms represented in the paintings and carvings of the great temple, which rises over the grove of mangoes and palms at the end of the street above the lotus-covered village tank. At half-past three or four in the afternoon the whole street is lighted up by the moving robes of the women going down to draw water from the tank, each with two or three water jars on her head: and so going and returning in single file, the scene glows like Titian's canvas, and moves like the stately procession of the Parthenaic frieze. Later the men drive in the mild grey kine from the jungle, the looms are folded up, the copper-smiths are silent, the elders gather in the gate, the lights begin to glimmer in the fast falling darkness, the feasting and the music begin, and the songs are sung late into the night from the *Ramayana* or *Mahabharata*. The next morning with sunrise, after simple ablutions and adorations performed in the open air before their houses, their same day begins again.'

English history books speak of the 'domestic' organization of the crafts prior to the Industrial Revolution. Reference to Defoe's travels alone will explode the idea that industry was carried from the fireside to the factory at one stride. Pre-Raphaelite sentimentalism has obscured the fact that all over the world civilization is based on organized industry; the American pioneering ideal of the self-supporting household gave way when the first trader opened his store. In Cobbett's hand that ideal became

[168]

a doctrine of self-reliance for the English working-man. He and his wife were to brew and bake for themselves and eat their own bacon, while the girls could plait their bonnets, because it was English and good to do so. Potatoes and tea were foreign and bad. It was left to Ruskin, as Professor of Art in Oxford University, to speak of the dignity of labour and to find something necessarily superior in the hand-made as against the machine-made. The average Indian village in the Deccan is founded on the existence of hereditary village servants, the carpenter, iron-smith and potter, among others, who may include priests of various kinds, the Mullah, if there is need of one, an astrologer and a hail-scarer. These basic specialists were necessary to the community and those that are still necessary have survived. A village of average size has only one carpenter and iron-smith, for his services are sufficient. They are repaid in kind with the traditional allowance of grain from each household. It is a fact, however, that many small villages have no potter and have to look to the market-town, where it is necessary to pay cash. Weaving and metal-work, other than simple iron forging, have always been market-town crafts, and, from the villager's point of view, a matter of cash, not kind. Spinning is done at home and simple white cloth of the *khaddar* type is sometimes woven by someone who owns fields and is really a farmer. The iron-smith makes ploughshares, reaping and weeding hooks, knives of various kinds, locks and needles. The carpenter makes ploughs, harrows, clod-crushers, seed-drills and big and little carts for the farmers, squares the uprights and transoms for house-building and produces doors, window-frames, beds, stools and cupboards. The potter makes the pots of the traditional size and shape which are customary in the neighbourhood. He may make a few toys for the children, horses and carts, cows, goats or bird-chariots. If it is customary he will make little ritual figurines of the local god or goddess. They are usually of the goddess: the goddess of child-birth or the Great Goddess-mother, whose local festival is held in the customary form of a fair with side-shows. He will also make little clay lamps that are lit before the Hindu shrines or Muslim tombs.

FIGURE 15

Ajanta fresco. 1st century B.C.

To ascribe a purely utilitarian function to the village craftsman is an over-simplification of the facts. To admit that the potter's toys are charming and that many of his pottery forms are delightful is beside the point; they were not made for the Western æsthete's enjoyment, but for the village. All that can be said is that this sort of life, far from being utilitarian, is in many ways extravagant.

[170]

Where the Western housewife must put up with jugs and basins of a few standard types, the villager's wife is accustomed to having a special pot to her hand for almost every special purpose, and the potter is willing and able to turn them out for her. It is extravagance for a farmer of few and poor acres to decorate his bullock's horns with gay silken tassels and dye their dewlaps magenta, or to spend five years' earnings on his daughter's marriage, or to leave his land and go to Benares or Rameshvaram on pilgrimage. But these things are all commonly done and are to be counted among the pleasures of life, which, after all, are few and far between. The fact that jewellery is a traditional form of wealth and that a man will hang his earnings round his wife's neck and arms and ankles is not merely to be regarded as an unsocial antiquated form of hoarding. It is delightful and until the new world with its Co-operative Societies and schools can give equivalent value in delight, it will certainly go on.

Between the villages and the market-town lies the kind of Indian road which is so aptly described as 'fair-weather'. Between the towns and the cities run the modern, engineered roads with their buses and lorries. Between city and city run the railways. What the villager cannot get at home, he must get in a market; what the town-dweller cannot get at home, he must buy in the cities. Each has its commodity: Jaipur jewellery, Benares brocades and mangoes, Peshawar turbans, embroidered shoes and serviceable grey cottons, dyed with the leaves of the scrubby palms, which cover the slopes of the frontier hills. Many of these special crafts are very old; Benares silks are mentioned in the Buddhist *Jatakas*. They have their own traditions; the patterns used being derived as much from the technique implicated as from any extraneous ideas of style. But generally speaking, such

[171]

things are luxuries, produced for those who can pay for them. You will not find them in village India.

What place, then, has art in the village? The drawing of lucky designs before the threshold is still common in many parts of India and the designs used are of great antiquity; the making of garlands, and decorated gateways for a marriage or a feast are universal. It may be that these are merely anthropological embellishments for which it is hard to find a place in the æsthetics of the West, but so it is. Embroidery is the supreme art of village India. You cannot have colour in textiles without the dyer's art and all other textile arts owe their being to his skill. Here the living taste of the countryside is, indeed, made manifest: the warm red-browns, beloved of the Kunbi women of the Deccan, being set beside the blue head-scarves and yellow skirts of the Delhi Jatnis, the soft tie-and-dyed fabrics of Rajputana beside the most ancient tradition of wearing white in Madras and the Dravidian south. Upon this basic colour-chart, embroidery draws its designs, which tell not only of differences between region and region, but between people and people. The satin-stitch *phulkaris* of the Panjab are unique and unmistakable, like the chain-stitch work on silk of Kacch and Kathiawar and the cross-stitch work of Sind. It is a slow and painful art and doubtless the time devoted to it might be spent more profitably. But it is delightful and, as work well done, a source of justifiable pride to the doer, and contributes greatly to the colour and beauty of the land, as anyone who has found time to sit by an Indian road-side will admit.

Like the lucky threshold patterns, embroidery belongs to the house and the women of the house. Materials have degenerated, both dyes and silks, and the younger generation has little patience for such things. But the designs have not degenerated as those of the commercial crafts of

[172]

the cities have. The work is done for its own sake and
will not change while it goes on. In most districts, however, it is undoubtedly dying. It would seem that certain
of the old arts have died, not because of the perfection of
modern machinery or of industrial exploitation of any
kind, but because people no longer have time for them.
Experience shows that once dead, they are dead for ever.

It may, then, be suggested that in the place of the naïve
opposition of the Fine Arts and the Industrial Arts, it is
advisable to discuss each art according to the need it
fulfils. The women will do their embroidery as long as
they have a need for doing it and possessing it. Of all the
arts, these old women's crafts alone are valued for themselves. The village crafts are open to development and
change; for instance, the village carpenter has come to
appreciate Western tools and to rely on screws and imported nails. The crafts of the rural market-town provide
for the needs of the farmer which the village cannot cope
with, and these change with time. Some of them are basic
necessities; shoes, for instance, are commonly market-
town products. But with the change to cash-transac-
tions fashion creeps in, though there is little margin
for luxuries in the country. The special manufactures of
the big cities are almost all luxuries for city or town use,
and as such are frankly the creatures of fashion. It is
interesting to note that these minor arts, many of them
borrowed from the Persian court by the Mughal court,
and from Delhi, Agra and Lahore by the petty Rajas of the
rustic provinces, were not regarded as distinct from the
Fine Arts. At the Mughal court, painting took its place by
the skilled, essentially luxury, crafts of the workers in
jade and crystal and the weavers of fine carpets. These
were never decentralized, but lived on as long as they
found a place in rich men's houses. When they became

too expensive, they died. Unlike the women's crafts, it has proved possible to resuscitate these high luxury crafts. The art-dealer has recently found it profitable to have copies made of the old Mughal jades and crystals, and has found craftsmen able to do the work and a ready market among those who must have their art embellished with the romance of pseudo-history.

4. THE CRAFTS OF THE PAST

At many ancient sites in northern India, seals of various guilds and corporations have been found in large numbers. There is an inscription at Sanchi recording the dedication of a bas-relief by the Guild of the Ivory Workers of the nearby city of Videsha. An Indian ivory figurine of the first century A.D. has been found at Pompei and there is a fragment of a carved ivory comb in the Victoria and Albert Museum. In A.D. 437–8, a temple dedicated to the Sun God was built in Malava by a company of silk weavers who had migrated to Mandasor from the Lata district. It was repaired in A.D. 473–4 and the inscription recording the pious act throws much light on craft conditions at that date.[1] It appears that some of the company abandoned their professional calling for other work. Others continued as weavers and the inscription describes their work: 'Just as a woman, though endowed with youth and beauty and adorned with golden necklaces and betel-leaves and flowers, does not go to meet her lover in a secret place, until she has put on a pair of silken cloths, so the whole of this region of the earth is adorned by the silk-weavers as if with a garment of silk, agreeable to the touch, variegated in colour, pleasing to the eye. . . .'

India has always been famed for its textiles and the

[1] Indian Art, Vol. XV, P. 194.

history of the craft typifies all other Indian crafts. The textile-trade has always been local, the trade names of the fabrics often preserving the name of their place of manufacture. *Calico* gets its name from Calicut and *shawl, chintz* and *bandana* are all Indian words. It is certain that India was, from the earliest times, a centre of the linked crafts of spinning, dyeing and weaving. Cotton has been found in Mohenjo-Daro and there are many references in the *Vedas* to weaving. In the *Amarakosa,* which probably dates from the fifth century, lists of technical terms are given, bearing upon costume and weaving, but it is not easy to arrive at their meaning. Bark, cotton-like fibres, various kinds of silks and *rankava* wool were in use. *Rankava* is interpreted in the commentaries as being the wool of deer, which does not exist, but is probably the *Pashmina* goat-wool from the north, from which shawls are still made. To the Chinese wearers of fine silks their western neighbours, who were wearers of wool and skins, were barbarians. India is undoubtedly the land of cotton-wearers, though silk was certainly used from early times. Sheep's wool and woollen materials seem never to have found a real place in ancient India, being regarded as dirty and suitable only for outer garments. They, too, probably belong to the north and came in with one or other of the series of northern invaders, culminating in the great Kushan empire. Authors commonly speak of 'linen' as being used in India. Since linseed is widely grown and its sheets of sky-blue blossom are conspicuous in the fields, this is plausible, but inaccurate. In India, linseed is used only as an oil-seed, while north of Hindu Kush, the flax only is used for linen and the seed and its oil are neglected.

In the fresco-painting at Ajanta, illustrating the *Chadanta Jataka,* the wife of the elephant hunter wears a leaf skirt. These were worn by the Chenchus of the Kistna gorges and the Juwangs of Orissa within living memory. Indeed, until quite recently, the bark fabrics mentioned in the ancient texts were still procurable.[1]

The famous Chinese pilgrim, Hiuen-tsiang, who travelled in India in the early seventh century, says that in peninsular India sewn clothes were not worn, though in the north close-fitting jackets were used in the cold weather. At this period, the western Turks ruled from the Ili to the Indus and it is with them and with his native China that he draws his comparisons. He says that white was the commonest colour for clothing. In all of this his compatriot, I-Tsing, agrees with him. It is, however, not true that tailoring was unknown in ancient India, for one of the large railing figures at Bharhut is shown wearing a fully tailored coat.[2] The famous portrait statue of the great Kushan king, Kanishka, now in the Indian Museum, Calcutta, shows him as the authentic northerner he was, in long coat and heavy boots of felt or fur-lined leather, such as are still made in Yarkhand.

Under the Kushans, the Buddha figure was created, and at the same time, the first Jain and Brahmanical icons were made, and Sanskrit replaced Prakrit in the inscriptions. The Kushans must have favoured these radical changes. Moreover, they seem to have permanently influenced the institution of Indian kingship. The Gupta kings of the fifth century who are usually regarded as having brought about a rebirth of Indian nationalism, still wear the tailored coat and trousers of their foreign predecessors. The trousers are not of the loose *shalwar* kind, which are found in Gandharan sculpture and are still worn by the Pathans; the Gupta kings wear the typically Indian

[1] *Sterculia urens* and *Antiaris succedanea* were among the trees used.

[2] Bharhut-Cunningham, Pl. xxxii, Inscription No. 55.

churidar trousers, tightly fitting the lower leg and cut long so that they are worn gathered down the leg. In the Lyrist types of Samudragupta and the King-Sitting-at-Ease types of Chandragupta II, however, the king wears the loose Indian waist-cloth. Later kings abandoned the Kushan boots and trousers altogether, and even rode in the Indian waist-cloth. Henceforward, the old Central Asian costume survives only in figures of Surya, the sun god.

It is not until the end of the fifth century that we find any real material for reviewing the costume of ancient India. In the frescoed walls of the Ajanta Caves, the past still lives before our eyes, but it is not easy to interpret. The purpose of these paintings is to illustrate the Buddhism of the day, in which the personalities of the great Bodhisattvas of the Greater Vehicle were prominent. These Saviours are conceived as kings and even in the subjects taken from the *Former Lives of the Buddha* royal processions and retinues and court life are everywhere prominent. Everywhere the architecture shown is palace architecture. Only here and there is everyday life treated as when above the head of the great Bodhisattva, *Padmapani,* the painter shows branches of the flowering shrubs that still grow about the entrance of the caves, and the pigeons which still have their nests high above in the barren hillside.

The frescoes belong to Buddhism but the world and reality are not excluded. The details of jewellery are, on the whole, faithful and correspond, not only with what is written in the texts, but with what we know of the craft from the earlier sculpture. Metal mirrors with handles of Hellenistic type and others, with a central boss at the back, of Chinese type, are to be seen: examples of tanged mirrors have been excavated in southern India. Little toilet bottles and caskets corresponding in form to the little vessels turned from steatite

[177]

and mottled pot-stones, which are found at many ancient sites in the north, also occur. The relic-caskets of the Buddhist stupas were made in the same way and were often similar in form; a strange meeting of the hieratic and worldly. There is one example of a well-known surviving craft, that of the so-called *swami*-wear of Tanjore, in which silver repoussé decorative plates and figures of the gods are applied to copper *lotas* and water-pots. It is, however, clear that the piled-up, jewelled head-dresses of the Bodhisattvas belong to iconography and not to real life. They are heavenly beings, vehicles of grace and active saviours, before whom the many pilgrims who attended the annual festivals bowed in supplication and adoration. Iconography had already come to dominate sculpture and painting in mediæval India. It is interesting to note that the earthly kings and princely heroes of the old Buddhist tales, which still provided the artists with their main themes, also wear these complicated jewel-encrusted and pearl-hung crowns. The development of the ideals of Indian kingship and of devotion to a personal god, which Indian religious feeling clings to despite the colder metaphysics of the schools of philosophy, are closely interwoven.

At Ajanta, foreign fashions are everywhere evident. The retinues of servants and soldiers are dressed in tight-fitting coats with V-necks, trousers and boots. Even the dancing girls have strangely cut bodices and jackets. More than once the vessels used are also foreign, including gadrooned ewers of Sassanian type. The Gupta kings are shown on their coins as wearing muslin turbans and the *Harshacharita* speaks of muslin turbans and knotted turbans.[1] They do not appear at Ajanta. The explanation can

[1] Moti Chandra. *J., Ind. Soc. Or. Art.*, Vol. XII, 1944, p. 2.

only be that these are court scenes and that the courts of the Guptas and their allies, the Vakatakas, were open to foreign influence in the persons of imported slaves and mercenaries. The *Periplus of the Erythrean Sea* in the first century A.D. chronicles the importation into India, via Barygaza,[1] of costly silver vessels, singing boys, and young

CXVII. G 54

FIGURE 16

Court official and dancer. Ajanta fresco.

Early 6th century A.D.

girls for the king's court. Dr. Barnett in his translation of the Jain work, *Antagadadasao*,[2] draws attention to evidence for the continuation of the practice in this text. Greek, Parthian, Arab, Bactrian and Persian slaves are mentioned, and it is said that each wore foreign dress after the fashion of their own country.

[1]Modern *Broach*.   [2] London, 1907.

As the Chinese pilgrims pointed out, white was the ordinary wear in India, and the fashion persisted until recently in the south. In the south, also, cut and sewn garments were not worn in early days. A tied band was used to cover the breasts of married women, but bodices were unknown, and young girls did not cover the breasts at all. This custom was kept by the Tiyan women of Malayalam until recently, while the women of the Waddar people, who are wandering irrigation experts and general labourers, Telegu by origin, still do not wear the bodice or cover the breasts in any way. Many patterns of bodices are worn in India to-day, some of them, such as that worn by the Pardhi bucksnarers of the Deccan, with its pendant points, being an obvious survival from those depicted at Ajanta.

It has been said that skirts also are to be seen at Ajanta, but this is not so. Like the bodice, the full gathered skirt belongs to the north and the west of the Peninsula. In the south it is unknown, and in the Deccan only the Pardhi, who originally came from Gujarat, and the Lamami bullock-carriers, who come from Multan, wear it. Both the bodice and the skirt are associated with local embroidery styles, varying widely in design and technique, but sharing the common use of fragments of looking-glass stitched to the fabric like *paillettes*. Everywhere else in India the *sari* is the woman's dress and the *dhoti* the man's, though there are many distinctive ways of tying them.

Four surviving textile techniques can be recognized at Ajanta, all of which are certainly ancient in India. It is abundantly clear that sprigged designs or floral diapers were not in use. The commonest pattern consists of chevron bands, the adjoining colours merging into each other. This special effect is achieved by the technique of double tied-resist dyeing, in which the warp and weft are tied and dyed separately before weaving. The silk *patolas* of Baroda, used as wedding *saris*, are made like this and the craft is still alive. Elsewhere, all-over spots or small circles on a plain ground are seen. This is the result of the famous *bandana* tie-and-dye technique, in which each spot to be resisted is caught up between the finger and thumb and tied with thread before the cloth is dipped. The examples at Ajanta are very simple, but in Jaipur and elsewhere in Rajputana polychrome *bandanas* are still made in fine designs. On a screen hung with various fabrics, there is a scrolled design which corresponds to the gold-brocades (*kincobs*) made at Benares and Surat. The cloth of gold sold to Western merchants at Baghdad, and known for that reason as *baudekin* in England, was probably made in India, though another sort, the *tartarium* of Marco Polo, also came from the Far East via Tartary. The names of the surviving patterns still made at Benares are full of romance, 'moon and stars', 'sunshine and shade', 'nightingale's eyes', 'peacock's neck.'

Lastly, fine muslins, spotted, or simply figured, are to be seen. These are the Dacca muslins which were once famous throughout the world. Tavernier says that the Persian ambassador received on behalf of his master a jewelled coconut containing a muslin turban thirty yards long. Fine work like this demands a lightness of hand, both in the spinning and weaving, which cannot be reproduced by any machine. Such fine thread could only be spun in the rainy season, with the spindle resting on a shell; the spindle itself was weighted only with a pinch of wet clay, accurately controlling the tension. The setting of the warp required infinite patience and the actual weaving was correspondingly slow. Plain webs of different weights were sold under such names as 'running water', 'evening dew', 'woven air', but striped fabric (*dorias*), checkered designs (*charkana*) and figured designs (*sansani*) were also made. The fame of Dacca was world-wide, but it should not be forgotten that such things were once made all over India, at Nagpur, Arni and Nellore, Gwalior and Hyderabad, Rohtak, Hoshiarpur, Ludhiana and Delhi, and many other places.

Embroidery has its place at Ajanta. One man wears a closely cut coat, ornamented with diagonal bands of geese and another has a coat with geometric bands alternating with floral bands. These designs are vaguely reminiscent of Sassanian art, but they have no Indian parallels. One of the great surviving schools of embroidery is that of the Panjab *phulkari* work, done by the women of the Jat and kindred castes. The work is devoted to bedspreads and hangings for the house and, especially, the distinctive skirts and head-cloths of the everyday dress. It is done in white, yellow and green *filoselle* in satin stitch on coarse red-brown cotton stuff, the threads being carefully counted as the patterns are repeated. The patterns, themselves, are mainly geometric but the technique has been used to produce bold sprigged floral designs, necessarily formal from the stitch used. The same intrusion of floral patterns may be seen in the Scind embroideries; and it is carried into the realm of naturalism in the Kach work.

In order to explain the ubiquity of the sprigged floral devices of modern Indian textiles, it is necessary to turn to the fashions of the Mughal court, where Persian influence held full sway. It may seem surprising that phases of court taste should leave their mark upon the countryside. But it is so, not merely in India, but every-where. The Tyrolean peasant costume, which delights the heart of the tourist as rustically quaint, once was fashionable in Vienna and Munich. The Indian village is not isolated, or even parochial. India is a land of many languages, many faiths, many fashions. People of all sorts are to be seen upon her roads: news travels quickly. The peasant does not feel himself behind the times. Indeed, there is no parallel in India for the self-conscious distinction implied in our talk of 'yokels' and 'cockneys'.

5. MUGHALS AND EUROPEANS

It is significant that the reigns of Akbar, the great Mughal, and of Elizabeth of England, were approximately contemporary. Men, then, lived in an atmosphere of discovery, of new continents, new peoples and new ways of life. In the sixteenth century the world had suddenly grown large and the realization of its great extent had lent importance to the distant and strange. Under these circumstances, the two realms met. The interest was mutual. Sir Thomas Roe, that conscientious merchant-ambassador, sought to titivate the Emperor Jahangir's mind with 'toyes' made in England; not always successfully, however, for the mirrors and wooden figures of horses, etc., with which the Company provided him, did not always attract the Asiatic. But it is extraordinary what a motley array of odds and ends did attract them, ranging from Jahangir's English coach and four, complete with English coachman, to the picture of Diana, which 'this yere gave great content'.[1] Roe knew his market and his 'Advise for goods for Surat', written to the Company in London in 1617, is precise. It is worth while considering the items it sets out. India wanted from England 'broad cloathes, corrall, lead,

[1] *The Embassy of Sir Thomas Roe*, Oxford, 1926, p. 453.

vermillion, wine, hott waters, swordes, knives, glasses, great pearles, rubies, ballasses, cattes eyes, emrauldes, aggats, armlets made to lock onn with one joint, arras, cloath of gold and silver branched grograines or sattins, gold lace, chamblets, and shirtes of mail, so they be lyght arrowe proofe and neately made'. He adds—'and generally I give you this rule: whatsoever you send in this kinde must be made by Indian patternes . . . I have patternes of . . . embroidered coates . . . of the King of divers soortes sent you'. He regretfully points out that embroidered goods have fallen in value—'for they have learned by ours to do as well'.

This is foreign influence with a vengeance, and, as Roe admits, it had a certain effect upon the court arts. But it was no new thing at the Mughal court. When Islam came to India, it found the arts fully developed, that is to say, it found a tradition to its hand. Of course, many of India's products were already familiar in the Islamic world and must have been known even to the early Arab invaders. Mahmud of Ghazni who, it is some-times forgotten, was a scholar and patron of literature, cannot suppress his admiration of the buildings he pillaged so ruthlessly in the land of the unbelievers.

By the beginning of the thirteenth century, Kutb u'd-din Aibak and Sultan Altamsh had raised up Delhi to be the capital of Muslim India. That a new era is declared by cultural change, in fact, that it creates its own setting, is an axiom of human history. Islam created the mosque and the tomb that is a mosque. Already at Samarra, Bagh-dad and Cairo great buildings had been raised. But the position in India was different. India already had trained masons and an established architectural and decorative tradition. Both at Ajmir and Delhi, as well as at Daulatabad and Bijapur, the pillars of sacked Hindu temples form the

[184]

supporting members of the earliest Indian mosques. The façades and general appearance of these are Islamic, just as their plan is necessarily Islamic. In the earlier examples, all traces of Hindu sculpture are obliterated with plaster, but the need for decoration could not be denied. In it is evident the hand of the Hindu sculptors and masons employed by their conquerors. In India the architect built *en bloc*, leaving it to the sculptor to give form to the building—in fact, the master-sculptor is the architect. Islam had its own plans and purposes. In the mosques and tombs it caused to be created, form came to dominate mere decoration. However, from the Kutb Mosque at Delhi to Gulbarga and Bijapur in the south, the Indian contribution is evident in the carved scroll-work and the magnificent use to which the traditional Kufic inscriptions are put. The decorative richness of all these buildings is wholly Indian. The two traditions are seen to merge. It is from this conjunction of the monumental and purely decorative that the Indo-Islamic arts of the coming centuries grow.

But what is new and, to a certain extent, what is strange, has an attraction of its own. The first Mughal emperor, Babur, imported architects from Constantinople. When Akbar created Indian painting by employing painters from Herat and Samarkand, he opened a new world of art to India, for Persian painting, through its Mongol phase, has Chinese origins. On the walls of the so-called Turkish Sultana's house at Fathpur Sikri are to be seen the well-known Chinese plum blossom and conventional clouds. That direct contact with China also existed is proved by the wealth of contemporary Chinese porcelain that is still preserved in India and by the broken fragments of celadon and other wares found at Bijapur and on the camping grounds that mark the stages on the imperial trunk roads. Roe[1] more than once mentions the Mughal taste for *Chinoiserie*. He writes: 'Any faire China bedsteads, or cabinets or truncks of Japan are here rich presents. Lately the king of Bisampore sent . . . China wares and one figure of cristall which the king accepted more than *gold*'. Later the craze was to spread to Europe, to such a degree that the very name 'Chinese' acquired a special value and many Indian products were sold and bought as such. Even the matter-of-fact Dr. Johnson responded to the demand for oriental romance.

A second feature of the new art produced under the patronage of the later Mughal emperors was what is called in the schools 'naturalism'. If the term has any meaning, it denotes not merely a doctrine or manner, but a way of seeing, and springs from a certain, perhaps naïve, but quite sincere, interest in things as they are. The Mughals were neither barbarian nor provincial. They had behind them the technical and social graces of the great courts of Turkestan. Babur was a man of letters in his own right and had the seeing eye. He could write: 'I hunted one day on a hill that lies above Bajaur. The bison of this hill are black, except the tail which is of a different colour. The bison and deer of Hindustan are wholly dark coloured. . . . We caught a *sarik* bird. Its body was black as were its eyes.' He speaks of the beauty of the *Arghwan* blossom that still blooms in the little valleys above Kabul, which he loved so well, 'the yellow mingling with the red'.

Humayun, in exile, was concerned with other, and more worldly, matters, though he brought back much to India from the court of Shah Tahmasp, where he had found asylum. Here was laid the evident Persian foundations

---

[1] *Sir Thomas Roe, op. cit.,* p. 99.

of Mughal taste. It was left to Akbar to employ
Indian artists and to create a style. To Babur, India was
'ugly and detestable', and it is indeed proper that he
lies, as he wished, in Kabul among the hills that were
his true home. India was Akbar's home. His son, Jahangir, had his great-grandfather's realistic eye and it was
under him that the Mughal minor arts, as we know them,
came into being.

Western historians have chronicled his shortcomings.
He drank; he was lazy; he was cruel. But he could write:
'From the excellence of its sweet-scented flowers one
may prefer the fragrances of India to those of the flowers
of the whole world . . . The first is the *champa*—it has
the shape of the saffron flower, but is yellow inclining
to white. The tree is very symmetrical and large and full
of branches and leaves, and is very shady. . . . Surpassing
this even is the *keora*[1] . . . another is the *rae bel*, another
the *mulsari*[2]. . . . In attendance on my revered father,
I went to Pampur (in Kashmir) when the saffron was in
flower. On other plants in the world, first the stem
shoots and then the leaves and flowers. When the
saffron stem is four fingers breadth from the dry ground,
its flowers shoot out, of the colour of the iris, with four
petals and in the middle are four threads of orange
colour . . . of the length of a finger joint. . . . On Thurs-
day the 6th of the month my halting place was at Hatya.
On this road many *Palas*[3] trees were in bloom. The
flower is peculiar to Hindustan. It has no scent, but its
colour is flaming orange. The base of the flower is black.
. . . It is so beautiful that one cannot take one's eyes off
it. . . . It is not proved that in the inhabited world there
is such another place as Mandu . . . all that could be
written would still fall short of the many beauties of

[1] Pandanas.   [2] Mimusops.   [3] Butea.

that place. . . . I saw two things there that I had not seen in any other place in Hindustan. One was the tree of the wild plantain that grows in the wild corners of the fort, and the other was the nest of the *Mamula*, which is called in Persian *Dum-Sicha*.[1] Up till now none of the *shikaris* had pointed out its nest. By chance in the very building I was staying in, there was one with two young birds.'

The observation and the power of description are of the scientific order; the consuming interest of this man, who was also an emperor, echoes in every word. It was a sustained interest as is proved by his delightful account of the pairing and breeding of the tame *saras* cranes he kept as pets, which is interspersed in his register of state affairs, from the 14th of one month to the 25th of the next, when he records the appearance of the fledglings and the way they were fed by the mother-bird. Shahdara, where his tomb stands in a beautiful garden, is a fitting resting-place for one who wrote so much and so lovingly of the natural beauties of this world, so unnecessarily troubled by man's vagaries.

Jahangir's love of flowers is reflected in every phase of later Mughal art. The borders of the paintings of his reign are floral and naturalistic in intention, though it is evident that his court artists, while striving to meet his taste, had not the emperor's eye or knowledge, and consequently, few of the gay and delightful blossoms they painted are recognizable. Indeed, the whole thing rapidly became conventional, though the colours still live.

Jahangir's tomb at Shahdara is of white marble. This stone had been used for centuries as an embellishment, for instance, in the pierced windows of the Alai Darwaza at the Kutb. It now became the universal building stone. The male lines of the work in red sandstone of Akbar's

[1] Water Wagtail.

[188]

reign were lost in a new effeminacy, which soon gave way to palpable weakness. Shah Jahan's Hall of Audience at Agra is of white plaster, and tawdry to a degree. But whether in white marble or in plaster, all this architecture is only an excuse for applied decoration, gilded ribbon-work of European design being added to Jahangir's floral motives. The technique used was *pietra dura*, also an importation from the west.

The earliest Indian textiles we know are of Jahangir's reign; tent panels, embroidered in silk and gold on velvet, velvets painted in gold, the painted waist-cloths worn with official court dress, all are floral, delicate, delightful. But it is not usually recognized how new the style was, for in Akbar's reign the textile designs are checkered and striped with only occasional use of the well-known palmettes and lozenges of the universal Islamic tradition. These beautiful designs, with their flowing lines and soft colours, are entirely different from the contemporary products of the imperial carpet factories. Carpet knotting is a stubborn technique, which only yields slowly to changes of taste, though yield it did, as the great floral carpets made at Jaipur at the end of the century show.

A study of the paintings makes the change of style clear. It was under Jahangir and Shah Jahan that the designs we recognize as being specifically Indian came into being. The jewellery remained traditional: the many-stranded necklaces of pearls, large uncut stones with smaller pendant drops, the *sarpesh* turban ornaments, shaped like a plume or in the form of a peacock. But to this age-old craft, two new allied arts must be added: the cutting of wine cups, cosmetic boxes and rose-water sprinklers in jade and crystal. Roe mentions both jades and crystals as rarities and as late as Aurangzeb's reign, the astute Doctor Manucci was able to pass glass off as crystal, which he says was prohibitively expensive in India. Small wine cups were made of jade in Jahangir's reign, at least three of those he personally used having survived. But it was under Shah Jahan that the Indian lapidaries learnt to mould the hard stone freely to the contemporary taste. Some of these jades and crystals are cut with lilies or rose-like clusters; some are inlaid with jewels, rubies, white topaz and turquoise. Their grace and fragility embody the spirit of the age, an age about which it was left to Barnier to tell the truth.

Meanwhile, Roe and the western adventurers, Portuguese, Dutch, French and English, including the Jesuit fathers, had brought the West to the East. Inlaid writing-boxes of European form became fashionable, were copied and have survived in large numbers. The European art of marquetry was acquired; the Mass-table made for the Jesuits at Lahore is at South Kensington. Exports from India to the West are, however, more difficult to trace, beyond the spices and rare woods of the bills of lading.

Some Indian textiles had reached Europe in the early days of contact; in England the much admired Indian cottons were, first of all, imitated in wool. Later, Indian cotton came to dominate the East-India trade and the English woollen manufacturers had to seek protection from the new craze. The story of the interaction of Indian skill and the demands of western fashion is embodied in the large numbers of Indian *palampores,* which were imported into Europe from the end of the seventeenth century to the beginning of the nineteenth. A *palampore* is a bed-spread and they were used as such in England and on the Continent, though it appears that when they had served their purpose and became a little worn, it was customary to cut them up and make loose-bodied gowns of them, of which a number exist. The earliest examples are embroidered, using hard-spun silks and chain-stitch. The designs are all based on the well-known vase-and-flowers or flowering-tree motives, the details of the foliage and flowers showing clear evidence of contemporary Dutch and English influence.

Cotton painting was an old art in India, though the earliest examples surviving are the floral waist-cloths of Shah Jahan's reign. The patterns were pounced, but the painting of both dye and mordant and the wax resists used is free-hand, and so accurate that close examination is required to detect the variations. This is the art which gave the term *chintz* to the English market; chintz meaning *painted* and not *printed*. It was only later on that the laborious and expensive painted work came to be imitated by printing with wood-blocks. It is not certain when calico-printing became general in India. At Fostat, certain printed designs have been described as being possibly Indian, but, if they are, they must be pre-Mughal, and nothing of the kind has survived in India; nor do the Mughal paintings of Akbar's reign show anything that suggests printing. In modern India, many of the master-printers admit Persian origins, and it is possible that the art came from Persia in Jahangir's or Shah Jahan's reigns, along with other crafts, including that of the lacquer-work and shawl-weaving, which survived in Kashmir.

The great painted bed-spreads provide a magnificent array of designs, reflecting various phases of European taste throughout the eighteenth century. English sprigged designs of Queen Anne's reign are followed by French ribboned swag designs, while what must be almost the last of the series have Napoleonic sphinxes and neo-classical columns. They were, however, not made only for the West, for certain of them are based on Siamese designs, and Japanese influence is also found.

In the nineteenth century, Manchester captured the eastern markets with its cotton prints, and the Indian master-weaver was faced by a competition he could not cope with alone. He was not only undercut by Manchester, but was deserted by his patrons. The surviving princes were all for the foreign and the modern, as, indeed, was the Brahmin, Ram Mohun Roy. The Orientalists, a body of English scholars, defended Indian culture and pleaded for the past; Henry Lawrence dreamed of an Indian India, in which the future should grow from the past. But it was Macaulay, writing in his office in Calcutta, with the windows closed to keep out the noise of the Indian crowd, who was listened to, and it was the efficient and unimaginative John Lawrence who became Viceroy of India. The intention of the Great Exhibition was woefully fulfilled. But the last phase did not come, till India adopted Manchester's technique and, at one stroke, acquired mills, *chauls* and a new problem, that of un-skilled, mass labour.

One fact must be recorded to Manchester's credit. Forbes Watson, in 1873, was enabled to publish his magnificent series of volumes entitled: *The Textile Fabrics of India*. Manchester was willing to copy the old designs and so to keep them alive. The Indian mill-owner has not shown so much discrimination. Under such conditions, it is not only an industry, and the skill embodied in it, that dies, but taste and the live appreciation which is taste. Who can be the patron of art but the man of taste? And if there are no patrons of art, how can art live? The new India, rightly, looks to the future, but there is still matter for consideration in the past. Art does not spring up fully fledged. It cannot be created in a day. It grows, and appreciation is its breath of life.

INDEX

PLATES

PLATES

1. INDUS VALLEY (HARAPPA) PERIOD, CIRCA 2500 B.C.

(a) and (b) Male torso. Red sandstone. From Harappa. H. 3½ in.
(c) Torso of male dancer. Steatite. From Harappa. H. 4 in.
(d) Dancing girl. Bronze casting. From Mohenjo-daro. H. 4¼ in.
(e) Seal depicting Brahmani bull. 1½ by 1½ in. Steatite. From Mohenjo-daro.

(Photographs: Archaeological Survey of India)

2. MAURYAN PERIOD, 4TH-3RD CENTURY B.C.

(a) Male figure. Polished sandstone. From Parkham, U.P. H. 6 ft. 7 in.
(b) Male figure. Polished sandstone. From Patna, Bihar. H. 3 ft. 7 in.
(c) Capital of Asokan pillar. Polished sandstone. From Sarnath. H. 6 ft.

(Photographs: Archaeological Survey of India)

3. YAKSHIS CARVED ON THE RAILING, BHARHUT STUPA, 2ND CENTURY B.C.

H. 6 ft. 3 in.

(Photographs: Archaeological Survev of India)

[197]

4. EASTERN GATE OF THE GREAT STUPA, SANCHI. 1ST CENTURY B.C.

   (*Photograph : Archaeological Survey of India*)

5. GANDHARA AND GUPTA SCULPTURE, 3RD-6TH CENTURY A.D.

   (a) The Buddha. Slate. From Gandhara, N.W. India. 3rd-5th century A.D.

   (*Haughton Collection*)

   (b) Torso of standing Buddha. Red sandstone. Gupta Period, 5th-6th century A.D. From Mathura. H. 2 ft. 10 in.

   (*Curzon Museum, Mathura*)

   (c) Torso of Bodhisattva. Sandstone. Gupta Period, 4th-5th century A.D. From Sanchi. H. 2 ft. 10 in.

   (*Victoria and Albert Museum*)

6. A BODHISATTVA. COPY BY GRIFFITHS OF WALL-PAINTING, VESTIBULE OF CAVE I, AJANTA. 6TH CENTURY A.D.

   (*Victoria and Albert Museum*)

7. ROCK-CUT FIGURES AT THE KAILASA TEMPLE, ELLORA, 8TH CENTURY A.D.

   (a) Siva as the Destroyer
   (b) Siva as the Divine Dancer

   (*Photographs: K. de B. Codrington*)

8. SCULPTURE AT THE KONARAK TEMPLE, ORISSA. 13TH CENTURY A.D.

   (a) Figure of musician on the roof

(b) Carving at the site of the north gate
(Photographs: John Irwin)

9. NATARAJA (SIVA AS LORD OF THE DANCE)

Bronze casting. From Madras Presidency, 11th century A.D. H. 3 ft.
(Victoria and Albert Museum)

10. AKBAR'S ENTRY INTO SURAT, 1572

Artist: Farrukh Beg. Mughal school: late 16th century. Page from an illustrated MS. of the *Akbar-nama*
(Victoria and Albert Museum)

11. PRINCE DARA SHIKOH ON THE IMPERIAL ELEPHANT NAMED MAHABIR DEB

Brush drawing on paper. Mughal school: about 1630 (or perhaps later)
(Victoria and Albert Museum)

12. A DERVISH, A SOLDIER, AND A MUSICIAN, IN A LANDSCAPE

Mughal school: mid-seventeenth century
(Chester Beatty Collection)

13. A LADY WITH ATTENDANTS

Unfinished drawing. Kangra school: about 1800
(Collection of J. C. French, Esq.)

14. A PRINCE AND OTHERS IN A GARDEN

Artist: Rahim ' Dakani '. Deccan school: late 17th century
(Chester Beatty Collection)

15. CEREMONIAL GIRDLE (PATKA)

Cotton, drawn and painted by hand. Mughal: 17th century

(*Victoria and Albert Museum*)

16. (a) Bowl. Crystal. Mughal: 17th century
    (b) Turban ornament. Jade, gold and jewellery. Mughal: 17th century
    (c) Turban ornament. Gold and enamelling. From Jaipur, Rajputana. Mughal: 17th century

(*Victoria and Albert Museum*)

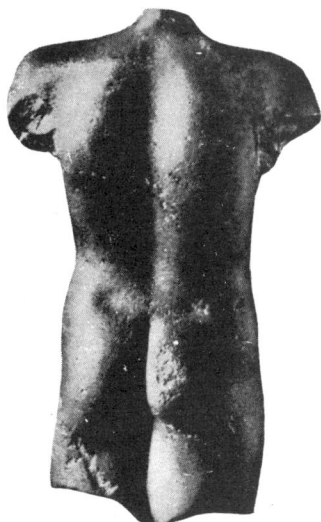

a

b

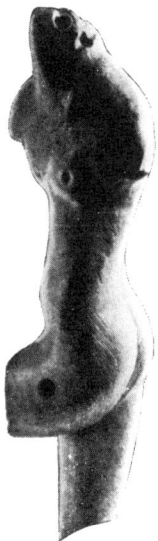

c

d

e

PLATE I

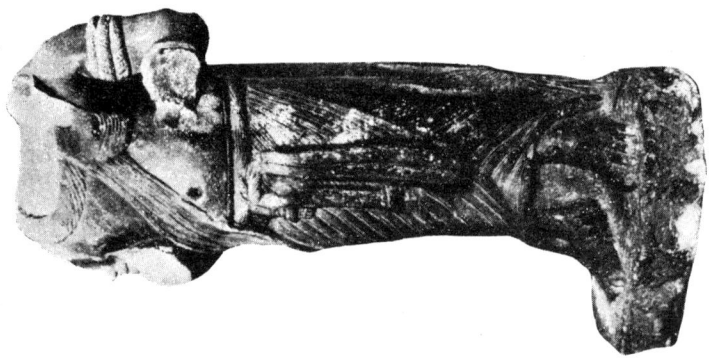

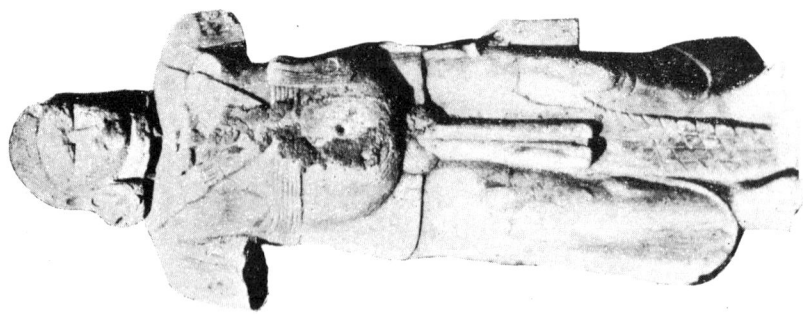

a

b

c

PLATE II

a

b

PLATE III

PLATE IV

PLATE V

a   b   c

PLATE VI

a

b

PLATE VII

PLATE VIII

PLATE IX

PLATE X

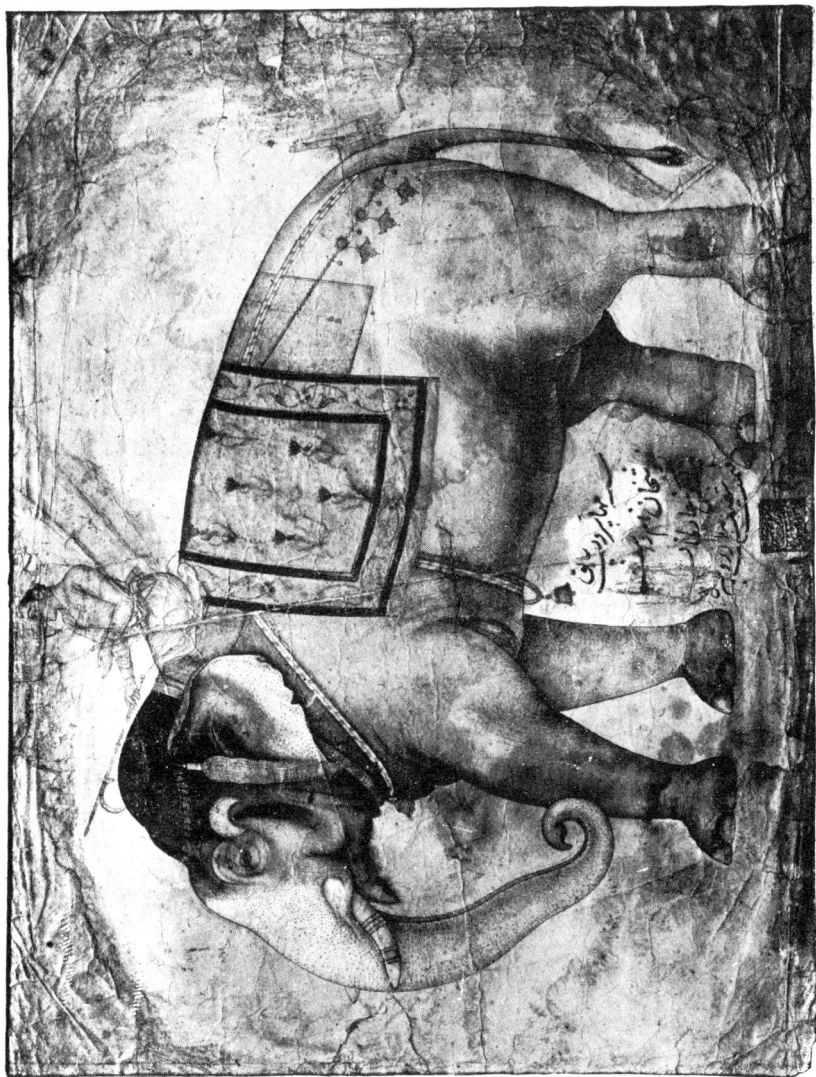

PLATE XI

PLATE XII

PLATE XIII

PLATE XIV

PLATE XV

a

b

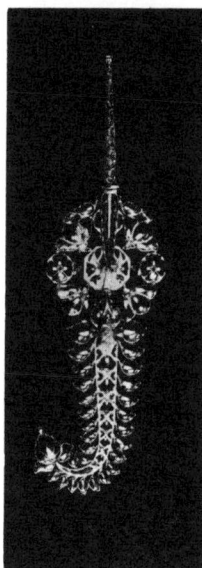

c

PLATE XVI